D0610588

PRAYER MO

By the same author and published by Kingsway:
Korea Miracle

Prayer Mountains

COLIN WHITTAKER

KINGSWAY
EASTBOURNE

Front cover design by Vic Mitchell

British Library Cataloguing in Publication Data

Whittaker, Colin
    Prayer Mountains.
    1.   South Korea. Christian Church. Growth
    I.   Title
    275.19'5

    ISBN 0-86065-772-8

Production and printing in Great Britain for
KINGSWAY PUBLICATIONS LTD
1 St Anne's Road, Eastbourne, E Sussex BN21 3UN by
Nuprint Ltd, 30b Station Road, Harpenden, Herts AL5 4SE.

Contents

Dedication

It is my great joy to dedicate this book to the elders emeritus and their wives, at The Mount of Olives Pentecostal Church: Fred and Maud Hankin, and Philip and Dora Allman. Fred and Philip are lovingly known to our fellowship as Mr Prayer and Mr. Praise. With their faithful wives they have given an example to all who have the courage and dedication to follow. The only reason they have ever missed a prayer meeting during my pastorate is because of sickness. 1989 is our Diamond Jubilee Year and Fred has been in the church almost from the beginning, and Philip almost as long. Whatever God has done in the church has been due to prayer.

Foreword

Edward England has become something of a phe-
nomenon in the world of Christian publishing. When he
suggested a book about prayer mountains, in view of
the growing interest in them, I very readily complied.
Having visited the International Prayer Mountain in
Korea, and having touched upon the subject in *Korea
Miracle*, I was delighted to have the opportunity to
pursue it further and more fully.

The three inter-related topics which lie nearest to my
heart are: prayer, revival and the working of the Holy
Spirit. It is a tremendous joy to witness the growing
army of prayer warriors around the world who are all
marching to the same drumbeat of worldwide revival in
our day.

It seems that prayer mountains are destined to play
an increasing role in achieving that goal. Until recently
they have been almost exclusively Korean in concept
and location. Now praying Christians in other lands
feel inspired to emulate the Korean example.

In writing this book I sent numerous letters to many
nations in an effort to gather as much information as
possible about the spread of prayer mountains. I was
especially thrilled when I finally tracked one down in
the Western world. I was informed that it belonged to

Evangel Christian Life Centre, Louisville, Kentucky, USA. In October 1988, I wrote to the founding pastor, Revd Wayne L Rodgers. Just as I was about to mail my completed manuscript to my publisher, I received this moving and touching reply from Wayne Rodgers' Associate Pastor, Greg Holt:

> I regret to inform you that Pastor W L Rodgers is unable to respond to you regarding information on Prayer Mountain (at this time) as he is rejoicing with the angels in heaven as of 2nd November 1988. I will, however, share with you my knowledge of Prayer Mountain.
>
> Prayer has always been an important part of Evangel Christian Life Centre. After going to Korea, Pastor W L Rodgers came home with a vision to have a similar place of refuge where people could come and fast and seek the face of God.
>
> Prayer Mountain is located on over four hundred acres of land in Brooks, Kentucky, about twenty minutes from downtown Louisville. The property has a lodge with sleeping quarters for both men and women. Prayer grottos are located in the side of the mountain which are used by individuals for prayer. There is a 1,500-foot ampitheatre, a parsonage in which the Director lives, and countless numbers of trails for people to walk and talk with the Lord.
>
> The testimonies are too numerous to mention. There have been many who have gone to Prayer Mountain seeking direction and found there life-changing experiences through the power of prayer. Prayer Mountain is visited by all denominations and the Holy Spirit has been outpoured to most mainline denominations.
>
> One experience concerns two Catholic Sisters who came to pray for guidance and wisdom. They received the baptism of the Holy Spirit and returned to their fellowship to spark revival.
>
> Many healings have taken place as people have hid themselves and found the secret place of the Most High.

Prayer Mountain is truly a place where the power of God can touch people's lives as they separate themselves to seek the Lord.

Sincerely yours, Greg Holt (Associate Pastor).

It seems my letter arrived just around the time of the 'home-call' of this praying pastor, Wayne Rodgers. What a marvellous legacy to leave behind—a functioning prayer mountain, open to believers from all denominations. I never had the privilege of meeting Wayne Rodgers, but it is safe to say that the trumpets must surely have sounded on the other side at his passing and that he must have had a joyous entrance into heaven.

As Doctor Martyn Lloyd-Jones observed: 'Prayer is the ultimate test of a man's true spiritual condition. There is nothing that tells the truth about us as Christian people so much as our prayer life. Everything we do in the Christian life is easier than prayer.' Anyone, therefore, who can help people to pray more effectively must be rendering the highest service of all.

In the last chapter I have tried to answer the question: 'Why can't we have a prayer mountain?' Why not, indeed? But whether that ever happens or not, if this book stirs and warms your heart to pray afresh, I shall feel more than recompensed.

I must thank the many who have helped me with their ready response of information to my enquiries. Once again I must record my extra special thanks to my dear wife, Hazel, my prayer partner extraordinary, for her unfailing love, support and patience during the writing of yet another book; and also my older daughter, Beryl, for her invaluable help once more with the manuscript.

Colin Whittaker

I

Transfigured Mountains

When Dr Paul Yonggi Cho, the pastor of the world's largest church, says: 'The person who has influenced me most is my mother-in-law,' it is important to understand that he is speaking seriously. In the West, mothers-in-law have had such a bad press and been the butt of so many jokes that at the first hearing we are tempted to smile in anticipation of the punch line. The fact of the matter is that she is one of the most outstanding women of prayer of this generation. Dr Cho first met her in Bible College when he was a very raw young student and she was a mature student almost twice his age, married and with quite a grown-up family. She soon recognised his potential and took him under her wing. He adds: 'She introduced me to the baptism of the Holy Spirit and prophesied over me that I would marry her daughter. It was this same woman who started Prayer Mountain and who played an unusual role in my early life and ministry.'

The lady in question, Dr Jashil Choi, is undoubtedly one of the great Christian women of influence of this

century. Although as yet her name is little known outside of her native Korea, the next generation will almost
certainly discover more of her greatness as the Korean
church continues its spectacular progress. The main
secret behind that growth is prayer. Korean Christians
have always taken their praying seriously, whereas the
average prayer meeting in Western churches has degenerated to the point where it is laughable—or it would
be if it did not reveal a lamentable state of affairs.
Fortunately, there are indications that this is changing.
Over the past few years faithful groups of believers in
the West have given themselves to seeking the face of
God in earnest and protracted praying. The result is
that the prayer meeting is no longer the Cinderella of
the church programme. The more people prevail, the
greater the interest becomes in rediscovering the secrets
of prayer in all of its many aspects. Indeed, the part
that prayer mountains play in Korean intercession is
really beginning to capture the imagination of intercessors in the West—hence this book. My visits to the
International Prayer Mountain will live with me for
ever.

Just when and where the idea of prayer mountains
originated is somewhat uncertain, but there is no doubt
whatsoever that the one person responsible more than
any other for exploiting the full potential of this concept
in our day is Dr Jashil Choi. She pioneered what is now
by far the biggest and most successful prayer mountain
in Korea where thousands can be found praying and
fasting every day of the year. It is surely no coincidence
that this particular prayer mountain is an inseparable
part of a church of over 600,000 members whose next
target is one million. Prayer still changes things at the
end of the twentieth century.

Prayer and mountains have been linked together since the beginning of time. Mountains and prayer, naturally and supernaturally, seem to have been just made for each other. The International Prayer Mountain of Yoido Full Gospel Church is a case in point. It is strategically placed in the attractive countryside near to the universally-known 38th Parallel, the cruel boundary which has divided Korea since the end of World War Two in 1945. Prayer Mountain is at Osanri, in the Kyunggi Province, virtually on the edge of the Demilitarised Zone which separates South Korea from Communist North Korea. Millions of Christians in South Korea believe that prayer is the only force great enough to ensure the continued freedom of their nation. (The proximity of this prayer mountain to the Communist North certainly gives an edge to their praying, since under the leadership of Kim Il Sung, North Korea has degenerated into what many consider to be one of the most ruthless, wretched and repressive regimes in the world today.) However, the praying at Prayer Mountain is not only concerned with keeping the communists at bay; these amazing people believe that one day, through their prayers (and their constant gospel broadcasts), the North will be taken 'peacefully' for Christ and the nation will be reunited.

Although the origin of prayer mountains is somewhat obscure, it must be made clear that there is nothing mystical or mysterious about the many prayer mountains in Korea and those in other countries which have resulted through their inspiration. Nearly all the prayer mountains in Korea are linked with and belong to sound and responsible churches. In essence they are simply quiet places set aside especially for prayer, for individuals and for groups of all sizes. The mountains in question had no spiritual significance before being set aside for intercession, neither are they now regarded as 'specially holy places' in themselves. Indeed, the sixty-acre site now occupied by the Yoido Full Gospel Church's International Prayer Mountain was originally a cemetery and was actually purchased for that purpose. It is situated less than thirty miles north of Seoul and only after Yonggi Cho had secured it did Dr Jashil Choi realise its potential. The concept gripped her and like another faith stalwart of old, she pleaded, 'Give me this mountain' (Josh 14:12). That was in the early 1970s, during a period of tremendous spiritual and financial pressure when they were building the massive new church sanctuary at Yoido. Not everyone, by any means, was in favour of turning the cemetery site into a prayer mountain and Dr Jashil Choi found herself with a mighty prayer battle on her hands to gain her objective.

She gave herself to prayer and fasting and visited the site daily for over three months, seeking the mind of God about it and desiring clear guidance as to the will of God in the matter. She wept and prayed, pouring out her very soul in earnest supplication, until after almost three months she received the sign she sought in the healing of a man who was dying of TB. The battle was won and it was agreed that the site would be set aside for a prayer mountain.

Dr Jashil Choi and other dedicated prayer warriors did not wait until the site was developed with permanent buildings before they gathered there to pray and fast. At first they made do with a tent, and every night for three years she was there praying until the first sanctuary on the site was opened on the 30th July 1974.

From a simple beginning with one praying woman it has developed into a place where there are prayer meetings every day of the year, with great numbers of people who have come for only one purpose—to pray. Furthermore, the prayer is constant not casual. You can guarantee you will always find there between 2,000 and 3,000 people praying. In addition, a large percentage of them will be fasting. At weekends numbers regularly swell to more than 10,000, and on special occasions crowds of around 20,000 throng the site. Yonggi Cho is a convinced believer in the power of organised prayer by great numbers. You cannot be in his presence very long before you will hear him declare with great conviction: 'If you don't involve your churches in mass prayer, you will never see revival. Prayer is the key to revival and church growth. You can have all kinds of gimmickry, but none of it will work if you do not pay the price. To bring revival you must pay the price. You must have massive organised prayer in your churches if you are to experience the miracle of church growth.'

If you want to see massive organised prayer being practised, then International Prayer Mountain is the place to visit. At the same time it must be stressed that the praying there is additional to the Full Gospel Church's regular intensive prayer programme at Yoido. That consists of all-night prayer meetings every night of the week, with at least 2,000 people each evening, and at the big one on Friday night they regularly exceed the 25,000 attendance figure. Furthermore, prayer is an integral and main part of the more than 50,000 house groups which meet every week.

There is a regular full-time staff of ministers and helpers who man Prayer Mountain around the clock and throughout the whole year. They have no problem in understanding Paul's exhortation to 'pray without ceasing'. Their biggest problem is stopping people once they have started praying, whereas ours is getting people to start! They are sometimes accused of neglecting their families through their devotion to prayer at Prayer Mountain, but by and large that is a carping criticism from a few who cannot understand how anyone can possibly pray for more than five minutes.

Most of the large, regular gatherings for prayer at Prayer Mountain are organised by one of the twenty-two district leaders. Some of these pastors are responsible for over 30,000 people in their district. The districts in turn are divided into sub-districts, each of which has its own pastoral leadership, and these are broken up into house cells—each of which has its own cell leader and assistant leader. The district leaders work together on a rota system to organise regular intercession at Prayer Mountain as well as nightly intercession at Yoido Full Gospel Church. This is a tremendous task, but there are 500 full-time, trained ministers to share the burden and they do have some 600,000 members to draw upon, not forgetting the 50,000 and more house-group leaders. A large percentage of these are women, who serve voluntarily in what virtually amounts to full-time service. (All of these know how to pray effectively and many of them are really outstanding prayer warriors as well as amazingly successful personal soul winners.)

It is a tremendous sight to see dozens of coaches arriving at Prayer Mountain bringing 2,000 or more from a district for a day's praying. They usually meet in one of the outer buildings and most of them sit on the floor, Korean fashion. (It is amusing to us Westerners to see some of the Koreans squat on the pews in the church rather than sit—they obviously find it more comfortable than sitting with their legs dangling. But be warned, it is an art that has been acquired only after many generations of practice. Westerners who try to emulate them and squat for hours on the floor tend to find themselves the victims of very painful attacks of cramp!)

In these district days (or nights) of prayer, the pattern usually followed is a fairly formal one consisting of a traditional hymn, the Lord's Prayer, more singing, the reciting of the Apostles' Creed, then prayer by the leader followed by a Bible-based exposition and exhortation. United prayer then follows, some of it from pastors on the platform who lead the great gathering into fervent prayer for definite needs, ranging from the needs of their own nation to worldwide missions; some of it is in the form of free congregational prayer focusing on some specific need which has been introduced from the platform. In these 'open' sessions of free prayer, all the congregation pray together. It is not a question of people in the congregation standing up one after another and praying, but all of them praying out loud, all together, all the time. Much of such praying is 'in the Spirit', that is 'in other tongues', but they pray 'with the understanding' also, in their own language. One has to experience the power of such intercession to appreciate it. Many Westerners find it disconcerting at first, especially those who are familiar only with very formal types of praying. However, this free, extempore praying in unison has been a unique feature of the Korean Revival since 1907.

One can now also encounter it in other Asian countries where God is pouring out his Spirit in revival blessing but it is something which is still very seldom experienced in the West. The strangeness of it though is probably with us rather than with them because many Bible students are of the opinion that something very similar must have happened on the occasion so graphically described by Luke in Acts where we read: 'They lifted up their voice to God with one accord' (4:24). The power of such praying can be judged by the results, in this case 'the place was shaken where they were assembled together; and they were all filled with the Holy Ghost, and they spake the word of God with boldness' (v 31).

To be in the midst of such praying at Prayer Mountain reminds me in some ways of a visit to Niagara we made en route to Korea. We took a trip on the boat called *Maid of the Mist* which takes tourists to the area immediately below the mighty Niagara Falls. On boarding the sturdy vessel, which can carry a hundred or so passengers, everyone was furnished with a blue, waterproof, monk-like garment complete with hood, which covered us from head to foot. We all stood on the open decks to view the magnificent spectacle. It was breathtaking and awe-inspiring to view the Falls from the river beneath. The captain headed the vessel from the Canadian side directly to the Horseshoe Falls. At first there was only the distant rumble of the deluging waters and the passage was quite smooth on the area of the river which had almost recovered its equilibrium after tumbling from great heights. Soon, however, the rumble changed into a roar, and the boat began to shake as the turbulent waters nearer the Falls battered its sides. The powerful engines of the boat responded magnificently and their beats became deep throbs from its brave heart which pulsated the very deck beneath our feet. On and on it ploughed through the white, foaming waters, which now attacked the sides of the boat in an absolute frenzy as though resenting any intrusion into this forbidden area at the foot of the Falls. By this time the roar of the waters had increased to a thunderous crescendo of noise which overwhelmed us. In spite of the protecting waterproofs we found ourselves getting soaked as the all-enclosing mist and spray joined forces with the maddened waters as though determined to overpower this intruding vessel if it dared to proceed any further. There came a frightening moment when the cacophony caused by the combined forces of the mighty Niagara in conflict with the furious pounding of the ship's engines made the vessel shake to the point where we felt that it was going to disintegrate under the strain. We instinctively wanted to cry out to the captain, 'Turn back! Turn back! Please turn back now....' The terror continued to grip us for a few more seconds and then what relief we felt when the boat began to turn and retreat to safety.

To be in the great gatherings at Prayer Mountain is a very similar experience. You find yourself engulfed in wave after wave of praying voices, which rise and fall only to rise again with ever greater noise and fervency. To gaze around brings no relief for you find yourself surrounded by a forest of hands which move ceaselessly, swaying and waving, a fervent physical expression of the intense intercession in which they are engaging. It is both frightening and challenging. When they pray for the salvation of lost souls it is clear that they really believe people will be lost for ever unless they receive the gospel of Christ's blood-bought redemption. Tears mingle with their prayers. Frequently their whole bodies sway backwards and forwards as they pour out their very beings in prayer. Others beat their knees with their fists as they battle against the Enemy of souls in spiritual warfare and seek to lay hold on God. At times it is so intense that you are relieved when, at the given signal of the ringing of a bell by the presiding pastor on the platform, the thousands instantly obey and within seconds there is perfect calm and quietness as they wait to receive their next prayer assignment.

Prayer Mountain is no place for the faint-hearted. It is a place where Christians understand what Paul is talking about when he commands Epaphras, one of their own pastors, to the Colossians because he is 'always labouring [or striving] fervently for [them] in prayers' (Col 4:12).

2

Transfigured People

Mass praying is spectacularly powerful, but the Lord
Jesus made it very clear in the first lesson of his prayer
school that we must learn the secret of getting alone
with God. In the world's most famous sermon he taught
his followers: 'When thou prayest, enter into thy closet,
and when thou hast shut thy door, pray to thy Father
which is in secret; and thy Father which seeth in secret
shall reward thee openly' (Mt 6:6).

They recognise this at International Prayer Mountain, where they make provision for private prayer in
the individual prayer grottos which are scattered all
over the location. There are some 150 of these cubicles
which are extremely basic and very small. These rough
concrete structures are cut into the side of the hill and
measure no more than five feet in height, width, or
length. This means that conditions are rather cramped,
to say the least, even for Koreans, who on average are
much smaller than Westerners. To my chagrin, once I
had entered and closed the door on myself, I found
them unbearably claustrophobic. Too small to stand up
in, too short to lie down in and too narrow for one to do

anything in comfort—except kneel down! They are completely devoid of all creature comforts. The walls are bare, as is the floor apart from a kneeling mat. There is no light and if you want any then you must take your own supply of candles and matches or a torch and a good supply of batteries. There are no windows and the candles are solely for light and have no sacramental significance. There is a small ventilation grill which allows in just about enough air to suffice. Nevertheless, in spite of that, it is almost impossible to find a vacant grotto.

Wander around the site and the shoes outside every grotto tell you that they are occupied. (It is the Korean custom for people to remove their shoes when entering a house.) Again this has nothing to do with religion as is the case with Muslims when they enter a mosque; in Korea this is purely a matter of hygiene. Most of their homes are still very small and living rooms frequently serve as bedrooms at night. Traditionally their homes are heated by underfloor heating systems so that in winter it guarantees a good warm bed. Shoes are removed on entering a Korean house for the same reason that it would be unthinkable for any guest in a Western home to walk all over the beds with their shoes on! As a matter of interest, Koreans keep their shoes on in church, but take them off before entering the grottos because many of them will be there for days at a time.

Walking around Prayer Mountain among the grottos one is soon made aware that while some are praying silently others are praying audibly—exceedingly so in many cases! On some days, because of its proximity to the border with North Korea, it is possible to hear the Communist propaganda which is being blasted out on loud speakers facing South Korea with the hope that people in the area will hear it. It is a totally wasted

effort so far as the Christians are concerned. Many of
them tasted life under the extreme Communist regime
of Kim Il Sung and fled South to freedom before the
border was finally sealed at the end of the Korean War
in 1953. Many of them are the children of Christian
parents who were martyred in North Korea in the dark
days between 1945 and 1950; the Korean War gave
them the opportunity to grasp at freedom and they took
it.

This is one explanation for their commitment to
prayer. They believe that prayer to the living God in
the name of his Son, Jesus Christ, is a million times
more powerful than propaganda. The many miracles
which take place at Prayer Mountain are abundant
proof that God does hear their prayers. These are directed heavenward, but one suspects that from time to
time, especially when the crowds swell to 20,000, those
across the border in North Korea hear the sound of
their mass praying and their marvellous hymn singing
and praise, and surely they must tremble! (Yoido Full
Gospel Church has operated a Communist Bloc Mission since 1986.)

Kim Il Sung has indoctrinated his people to believe
that they do not need God. The teaching called the
'Juche Idea' was celebrated by the erection of a 500-foot
tower to commemorate Kim's seventieth birthday. In
essence the Juche Idea is that man is his own master.
Man is the master of the world and of his own destiny.
His son, Kim Jong Il, is thirty-one years younger than
his father and has been carefully groomed to succeed
him. There is a statue of Kim Il Sung in every town and
children have to come and lay flowers before it as well
as worship him with songs. They have to thank Kim for
every meal. Adults have to wear his badge and make a

lifelong study of his writings. They are brain-washed from the cradle to the grave.

It is an interesting battle and the Christians are right in the middle of it. For it must be remembered that in spite of the tremendous growth of Christianity in South Korea, and in spite of the almost continuous revival, Christians are still in a minority and form only some 25% of the population. In South Korea they are out-numbered three to one; while among the North's 21,000,000 there are not supposed to be any Christians left—they were all 'removed' in the early years of the Communist take-over. Their avowed aim was to eradi-cate all traces of Christianity, and Christians were called upon to renounce their faith or face imprison-ment or even death. However, recent reports indicate that the word of God is penetrating the darkness and an underground church is beginning to emerge. There are some quite large groups of believers in country areas and a few scattered believers in the cities. Remember-ing what God has done by his Spirit in China in the last forty years, there is cause for hope, and Prayer Moun-tain, geographically and spiritually, is at the front line of the conflict.

Many of the people praying in the grottos have come to Prayer Mountain with a specific burden on their hearts and they are prepared to wait on God for the answer. People come from all over the world to pray there as well as from all over Korea and from all the main denominations. Figures of the various believers attending are interesting: those who visit most fre-quently are 42% Presbyterian, 16.5% Methodist, 13.2% Holiness, 13% Full Gospel and 5.6% Baptist. (Presbyterians and Methodists are the largest denominations in the country, although the Full Gospel are gaining ground rapidly.)

A brief analysis of the various needs which people pray for at the mountain is also revealing. Top of the list is the need for the Holy Spirit's baptism of power, second come church problems, third are family matters, and divine healing—quite surprisingly—comes only fourth. It shows a very healthy balance of sound spiritual values with the physical last not first.

In the fifteen years since the inception of International Prayer Mountain the catalogue of authenticated miracles and definite and indisputable answers to prayer is numbered not in the tens, or twenties, or hundreds, or even in the thousands, but in the tens of thousands. They cover medically confirmed cases of cancer, local revivals in churches, ministers whose ministries have been transformed through receiving a new anointing of the Holy Spirit's power on their lives, and the salvation of families. One story from the latter category will have to suffice for this chapter.

In 1980, a young American Assemblies of God minister in America, Revd Don Stamps, was preparing to go with his wife and family to Brazil as a missionary. They had been busy for eighteen months visiting different churches and had successfully raised support for their first four-year term in Brazil. Just four months before the date set for their departure, Don felt an increasing burden for his sixty-five-year-old parents, neither of whom were Christians. This was the only thing spoiling his joy at the prospect of answering God's call on his life to win souls for Christ in Brazil. He really gave himself to prayer to ask God what he should do. His parents were retired and settled in life. He knew that it would not be easy to win them at that stage of their lives. Somehow Satan's power had to be broken to bring them to Christ, but how?

It was during this time of burdened prayer for his parents that Don heard about the prayer mountain connected with Yonggi Cho's church in Korea. As he waited on God he felt a definite leading that he should go there to pray and fast for the salvation of his parents.

He booked a flight to Seoul without really knowing what to expect when he arrived there. He took a taxi from the airport to Yoido Full Gospel Church and they graciously supplied him with a room for the night (Koreans are enthusiastically hospitable). Next day they told him how to get to Prayer Mountain on one of the church buses. These are free and leave from the church. Once there he started to pray and fast for his parents' salvation. He found that the time seemed to pass slowly but he persisted in prayer. The days passed and sometimes he walked across the hills in the area crying out to God. At other times he got into his little prayer grotto dug out of the mountain, shut the door and prayed: 'Oh, my God, some way the power of Satan must be broken. I have to win my mother and father before I leave the United States. Help me some way.'

After a week of such praying the Lord revealed to him how he should approach his parents and what words he should speak to them. He knew that victory was close at hand and that somehow the dark powers of evil that had been placed against his parents were beginning to crumble. He continued to pray and fast for another three days. The one Sunday he was there happened to be Easter Sunday, which fell in the middle of his fast, and he spent it back in Yonggi Cho's great church in Yoido. Although he was impressed with the vast numbers it was their fervent praying that moved him most and he was made aware that this was the secret to what God was doing in Korea.

At the end of his ten days of praying and fasting, secure in the knowledge that God had heard his cries, he boarded the plane for America. He arrived back home late on Saturday night and rose early on Sunday morning and told his two young sons, Toby and Todd, aged ten and eight years, to accompany him as they were going to win Grandmother and Grandad to Jesus Christ.

Don told his sons that he needed their help in this great task, and they were going to have to pray. He instructed them that when they got to their grandparents' house they were to go up into the back bedroom, get on their knees and pray for Grandmother and Grandad while he talked to them about Jesus. The boys did exactly as he told them and he began talking to his parents about the Lord. He told them the simple story of Christ's love and death for them and their need of redemption because of sin. He spoke to them for about forty minutes and for the first time in his life he saw his mother and father bow their heads and accept Jesus Christ as their Saviour. His parents started attending a good church and serving God while Don and his family departed with great rejoicing to the mission field of Brazil. Understandably, Don declares that he will never forget his experience at Prayer Mountain, and that sentiment is echoed by tens of thousands of other visitors there.

Returning to the words of Christ on private prayer with which this chapter started, there are some vital lessons to be observed in these familiar words. If we rush by them we shall miss the deep truths which lie just beneath the surface. It will do us no harm to repeat them again in full and to read them prayerfully and slowly, asking the Holy Spirit to 'enlighten the eyes of our understanding' as we do so. 'When thou prayest, enter into thy closet, and when thou hast shut thy door, pray to thy Father which is in secret; and thy Father which seeth in secret shall reward thee openly' (Mt 6:6).

As that devout Bible teacher and man of God, A T Pierson, long ago observed:

> The word 'closet' is unusual. The original Greek word, *tameion*, is found only four times in the New Testament; in one place being rendered 'secret chambers' and in another 'storehouse', (Matthew 24:26 and Luke 12:24). The words here used seem undoubtedly adapted from the Septuagint version of Isaiah 26:20, 'Come, my people, enter thou into thy chambers and shut thy doors about thee.' The closet is simply a closed place, shut in for privacy, shut out from intrusion and interruption. Christ was speaking to a Jewish audience and to the Hebrew mind there was one place that was pre-eminently a secret chamber: it was that innermost court of the Tabernacle and Temple, where God specially dwelt, and which was known as the Holy of Holies. We now have the key to this first lesson of our Lord on Prayer. The closet is the Holy of Holies where the suppliant soul meets God alone and communes with Him at the blood-sprinkled mercy-seat. The highest act of prayer is impossible, unless and until the human suppliant deliberately seeks to *meet God absolutely alone*.[1]

There is no doubt that over and over again those outwardly unattractive, concrete grottos dotted around Prayer Mountain have been transformed into the very Holy of Holies to those devout souls who have learned the secret of taking time to get alone with God and stay there in his presence until they hear from heaven.

3

Fasting

Fasting is an integral part of International Prayer Mountain. It is a place where people can draw aside from the normal routine of life and give themselves to fasting and prayer without anyone thinking them strange. On any day of the year you can guarantee that there will always be scores of people fasting as well as praying. The fasts vary from a short one of just a day up to a very long and intensive one of forty days. The average, however, is for a week or ten days.

Most Western Christians gasp in disbelief at the idea of doing without food for a week, let alone six weeks. Announce a day of prayer and fasting in the average church in the West and you will be very fortunate if even half of those you like to count as 'fully committed' respond. The majority usually find themselves suddenly afflicted with a whole host of mysterious maladies which have a tendency to clear up just as amazingly the next day. You can also be certain that a hard core of dissidents in the congregation will not hide their disapproval. Caustic comments such as: 'I don't believe in fasting' (which allows for no further argument); 'Fasting is totally unnecessary'; 'I would do it, of course, but my husband must have his cooked lunch or he would never survive' (such husbands usually turn out to be fourteen stone plus!); 'I can't see the sense of it myself. I mean, what's the point?'; 'I can't concentrate on an empty stomach. All I can think about is my lunch'; 'I get a headache when I fast. I know, I tried it once years ago and I've never done it since. That kind of thing is not for me. In fact I think it's going too far'; 'A friend of mine once told me that a friend had told them about someone they had heard about who had been ill after fasting.'

Dr Jashil Choi strongly advocates the practice. It is one of the many secrets of prevailing prayer which she learned from her godly mother in the early days of the Korean Revival. I have told a good deal of her fascinating life in *Korea Miracle* (Kingsway 1988) and so I will not go into it in any detail here. However, a little of her background is essential in order to gain an appreciation of Prayer Mountain.

Her personal story is an epic of suffering as well as of success. She was born in the northern region of Korea in 1915. In those days the fire was still burning from the great 1907 Revival in spite of the opposition to Christianity by the Japanese who had occupied Korea in 1910. Jashil Choi was brought up a Buddhist, but she had a marvellous conversion as a child through creeping into a tent crusade out of curiosity. The meeting was conducted by a Korean evangelist who also exercised a ministry of divine healing, which was quite unusual in those days in Korea. When she saw people healed before her very eyes Jashil ran to fetch her mother who suffered greatly from migraines. The result was that her mother, as well as being wonderfully healed, was also gloriously converted and became a totally committed Christian and a devout woman of prayer. The spirit of prayer prevailed throughout the churches in and around Pyongyang in those years and Jashil's mother progressed until she was appointed the head deaconness in the Second Presbyterian Church in Pyongyang.

Jashil was a bright and gifted girl and succeeded in her ambition to become a nurse. Once qualified she showed the daring in her character by volunteering to serve in the northern border area where murderous Manchurian bandits were a constant hazard. She took her life in her hands, but her motive was money more than mercy—the pay was higher because of the risks. Unfortunately her ambition to become rich resulted in a cooling of her Christian zeal. Her godly mother warned her and prayed for her, but in this backslidden condition she fell in love with and married a handsome and clever young Korean naval officer. It was a difficult marriage.

The Japanese occupation of Korea ended with their defeat by the Allies in World War Two in 1945. Sadly, for the future of Korea, the Allies decided to divide the country at the 38th Parallel, with the Russians occupying the North while America and her Allies took the South. Jashil's husband had to flee for his life to the South; she and their children planned to follow him at the first opportunity. Months later the chance came and with her mother and children Jashil made a hair-raising escape from the North to the freedom of South Korea. It marked the beginning of a new chapter in her life, but many more heartaches lay ahead of her before she was renewed in her faith.

Her handsome husband was something of a womaniser and he went off with a younger woman, leaving her to care for her aging mother and bring up her young family alone. She confesses that during this period of her life her attitude was largely negative, and her faith almost gone, despite the twenty-five years in which she had held various positions in the church. Then her mother died, and a daughter was killed in an accident, and the pressure of life's responsibilities became so intense that she tried to commit suicide by starvation. She did not eat for twenty days but God mercifully intervened in a way which revealed his over-ruling care in her life. Unexpectedly she met an old friend who, after much persuasion, got her to attend an evangelistic crusade where the evangelist turned out to be the very one who had led her and her mother to the Lord all those years before.

The spell was broken. She yielded her life totally to the Lord and began to seek God with all her heart. It was now that God began to teach her those things which have made her a great woman of faith and prayer. She learned the secrets of fasting as well as praying and was healed of diabetes and insomnia. Even more importantly, God took away her begrudging spirit and removed the hatred from within her heart. At forty-one years of age, deserted by her husband but her faith restored in a new and unreserved commitment to Christ, she enrolled in the Assemblies of God Bible School in Seoul.

In the Bible School she met a raw young student who was young enough to be her son—Yonggi Cho. She taught him the secrets of rising early to pray. Twice when he was very ill she prayed him through it. After Bible School she co-pastored with Yonggi Cho a new pioneer tent church in the poorest area of Seoul out of which was destined to grow the largest church in the world.

For over ten long years she never ceased to pray and believe for the restoration of her husband. Her prayers were answered in a remarkable way and her repentant and renewed husband eventually became Yonggi Cho's right hand man in the growing church. He also carried out successful missionary work in Japan and remained true and a power for God until he died.

The founding of Prayer Mountain in 1973 marked a new chapter of power in the life of Jashil Choi as well as in the progress of the Yoido Full Gospel Church. The vision for Prayer Mountain was that it was to be a place where prayer was continually being offered. There was to be provision for people to pray *en masse*, unitedly in great numbers. Smaller and more intimate groups were also to be provided for, in the open air in summer, with benches and a leader's rostrum, and in small chapels in winter. Private prayer was to be catered for by the erection of scores of individual prayer grottos dug into the mountain side. With it all, people were to be taught and encouraged to fast as well as pray. There is no doubt that fasting has added another dimension to the praying at Prayer Mountain.

The regular staff there includes twenty full-time pastors. Between them on a rota basis they arrange for four prayer services and sessions throughout each day. They and other members of staff supervise those undertaking long fasts to ensure that no one goes to extremes—they are deeply committed but they are not fanatics. As the world witnessed during the 1988 Olympic Games in Seoul, the Koreans are fantastic organisers—and Prayer Mountain is no exception. The regular free bus service from the church in Seoul runs like clockwork and with the minimum of fuss. The buses always seem to be full of happy people who spill out joyfully and eagerly at the terminus and pass through the reception area to be 'booked in' for whatever period they have come.

The reputation of International Prayer Mountain has spread throughout the world, drawing more and more people of all nationalities. Nothing succeeds like success and there is nothing like answered prayer for getting people to pray. The more people see definite answers to their prayers, the more they desire to pray and the more other people want to join them. It is a chain reaction that is virtually unstoppable. That is why, from its humble beginning with Jashil Choi and a handful of prayer warriors meeting on the bare hillside in the early 1970s, it has now grown to a massive campus capable of catering for crowds of 20,000 plus.

They began with a tent and then the first permanent building was completed and dedicated on 30th July 1974. Within four short years growth necessitated the erection and opening in 1978 of a larger main sanctuary and, along with it, dormitory accommodation for the increasing number who wanted to stay for days and even weeks at a time. On 1st December 1985 its world-wide recognition led them to change the name to International Prayer Mountain. Since then more dormitory accommodation has been built and also a magnificent main sanctury in the design of a great ark and capable of seating 10,000 people. With two more chapels each holding 5,000 people, this constitutes the accommodation for 20,000, but in addition there are some seven smaller chapels. Dormitory accommodation is available for around 3,000 people; most of it is quite basic although some of the more recent constructions are much better furnished.

Not everyone, by any means, goes to fast as well as pray, and there is a cafeteria where a wide variety of food is available for purchase at very reasonable prices.

There is absolutely no compulsion for anyone to do anything. No one makes people pray; they pray because they want to and feel the need. No one forces people to fast. Those who fast do so because they choose to do so and because they have a burden on their hearts. They are free to break their fast at any time. The only time anyone on the staff would interfere would be in the case of a protracted fast where they felt there was a risk of someone overdoing it. Then they may well intervene in order to safeguard their good reputation. They would give guidance as to the correct way to break a long fast (ie very gently, beginning with diluted fruit juice and building up very slowly to solids) and would seek to help.

It is a very moving sight indeed to see several thousand people in the great main sanctuary and realise from the way that many of them are stretched out or kneeling on their blankets with their bottles of water, that hundreds of them are fasting. Many of them remain there day and night, moving only when it is necessary for them to visit the toilets and to wash. Koreans do seem to have a capacity for being able to sleep anywhere and at any time, but for the most part they seem to be able to manage on fairly little, so that they spend most of the time praying not sleeping. Many young mothers are there with their babies and toddlers and some of these mothers are fasting themselves but feeding their children. Outside, groups of older children can be seen occupying themselves, leaving parents free to concentrate on their praying. There is a good atmosphere at Prayer Mountain, with children laughing and playing, and parents and friends praying and praising, and others just strolling quietly around the hillsides and wooded paths, deep in meditation. In some of the great gatherings, intercession becomes very intense at times, and walking past some of the grottos it is obvious that some are 'groaning in the Spirit' and praying and weeping in agony of soul'—but generally there is plenty of joy and mostly a sense of victory prevails. Real fasting is soul travail, but even in fasting there are periods of release and freedom in the Spirit which more than compensate the denials involved.

Jashil Choi does not mince matters when preaching on the subject. She told me that she has spent over twenty years telling Christians to fast as well as pray, and when she started visiting Japan and giving them the fasting message they were very much against it. They asked her, 'Who told you to fast?' She told them that Moses fasted, as did the Lord Jesus and the church at Antioch. Joel the prophet called for a fast and so did Esther in a time of national emergency. She went on to tell them that she believed the Japanese needed to fast because of the scandal of the great numbers of their youths who committed suicide; and the Americans and Britains needed to fast because of the millions of abortions resulting in the murder of innocent unborn babies.

After she had been visiting Japan for two or three years, their opposition to fasting disappeared as they began to see the fruits of it. She believes that fasting breaks the yokes of satanic bondage; it also brings harmony among believers. During periods of fasting and waiting on God he gives revelation and power to witness, and the love of God is shed abroad in our hearts. The result is that miracles are experienced, empowered believers go out and pray for the sick, healings take place and the rivers of living water flow out just as Jesus promised. She claims that fasting has many beneficial physical side-effects and people who practise it regularly, as she herself does, tend to have strong bones and frequently find themselves healed of many minor (and some not so minor) infirmities. Through renewed health and spiritual quickening as a result of fasting, she also believes that we can bless our descendents physically and spiritually.

She will tell you that if you fast for just one day and spend lots of time 'eating' or 'devouring' or 'feeding' upon the word of God as well as praying, then you are giving your stomach a vacation, and the heart and liver and other organs also benefit. Your thinking becomes clear and your heart is filled with forgiveness.

However, she believes that when you fast for two or three days there is no one that you can hate. But if you fast for thirty days (as she has done a number of times) then you take pity on others who are sick. Furthermore, you are rejuvenated and filled with joy. She was seventy-three years of age when she told me this, and she said that she had just been examined by her doctor who told her that she had the body of a forty year old. When I met her she had preached every day for 130 days and the previous day she had been to a small village in the country and had preached for four hours!

There are many thousands of authenticated testimonies of miracles of healing of all kinds of diseases, and conversions and deliverances which have occurred at Prayer Mountain—proof sufficient for all but the most hardened and unreasonable sceptic whom nothing would convince. A few samples drawn at random will give some idea of the scope of the wonderful happenings which are a constant occurrence.

A Christian lady had suffered for twenty-eight years with a disease which was gradually paralysing her. She had medical treatment including acupuncture for three months without any improvement. Her family wanted her to go to hospital but instead she chose to go to Prayer Mountain to pray and fast for ten days. She was completely healed. When her backslidden daughter (who had married an unbeliever) saw what God had done for her they both yielded their lives to Christ. It was not long before her son-in-law went to Bible College and then became a pastor.

Another lady was in deep despair when breast cancer was diagnosed. The hospital told her that it was in an advanced stage and the only hope was surgery. She decided against the operation and returned home after receiving radiation treatment. Eventually she visited Yoido Full Gospel Church where Yonggi Cho prayed for her. She then decided to go to Prayer Mountain with her sister and pray and fast for a week. After four days she was completely healed and as a result totally rededicated her life to the Lord.

Yet another lady had suffered with terrible sores in her mouth for over twenty years. Hospital treatment and various medicines had been ineffective. She grew worse and was in constant pain. Her friends urged her to attend church but she resisted. Eventually, knowing that she was dying, she ventured out to Prayer Mountain. As she listened to the many testimonies of healing, hope was born within her and soon she decided to pray and fast for nine days. On the first day of her fast she confessed her sins and came to the Lord as Saviour. On the third day the sores in her mouth began to heal and soon she was completely healed.

The father of a Christian young man was suffering with stomach cancer. Hospital treatment produced no improvement and he was in despair. His son testified to him that many miracles happened at Prayer Mountain and if he would go there and pray and believe on Jesus he would be healed. The father had never heard of Jesus up to this time but under his son's constant urging he finally went. The singing, the worship, the

preaching were all strange to him but as he listened to
the testimonies of salvation and healing, faith began to
grow in his heart as he realised that from Jesus he could
receive healing for soul and body. He realised that he
was a sinner, so he repented and accepted Christ. He
began to seek God and although he was tempted to
smoke and eat he sought God more earnestly and over-
came the temptation. After fasting and praying for a
week he discharged a dark, red blood mass and the root
of the cancer. His joy and happiness knew no bounds.
He returned home saved, healed and determined to
praise and serve God for the rest of his life.

Dr Jashil Choi met a young man who had just gradu-
ated from Bible College. She urged him to seek the
power of the Holy Spirit right at the beginning of his
ministry. He went to Prayer Mountain to pray and fast
for ten days. It was his first fast of more than two days
but God helped him and met with him as he prayed for
God's blessing on his pioneer church. Soon he had the
joy of seeing fifty souls come to Christ under his ministry and he found the power of God resting upon his
ministry everywhere he went.

Jashil Choi and International Prayer Mountain are
two very good reasons for believing in fasting and
praying.

4

Hungering for God

The fasting prayer has been called 'atomic power with God' by those who have practised it and experienced its dynamism. One dedicated pastor in Hong Kong, has made over 400 trips from there into Red China over the last twenty years, carrying Bibles and ministering to the 'unofficial' churches. (His name is withheld for reasons of safety—the situation in China is still very precarious for Westerners.) One of the keys to the release of the miracle-working power of God in China today is prevailing prayer plus the added power dimension of fasting. It is to this pastor that I am indebted for this story of one of the house-church movement leaders in China who has just recently been released after four years in prison for preaching the gospel. During one part of his imprisonment he fasted for seventy days. A fast of such a duration is very unusual, though not unknown, and certainly is not to be recommended to the uninitiated. However, the outcome of this amazing fast was that this servant of the Lord had the joy of leading all the prisoners to Christ. When he finally broke his fast he asked the guards if he could have some bread and grape juice so that he could have Communion with these new converts. Since his release God's anointing has continued to rest upon this man of God in such power that he and his co-workers are now baptising scores of new converts every night.

Fasting is taught very positively at International Prayer Mountain and some do undertake fasts of forty days while there, but fasts of such duration are not encouraged and are allowed only in exceptional cases and then they are carefully supervised. They know only too well from experience that a few misguided fanatics can bring the whole subject of fasting into disrepute. Dr Jashil Choi and Dr Paul Yonggi Cho teach their people to start with short fasts of no more than three days. Once they have done this several times the fear of fasting is largely removed and most are then quite eager to try a fast of one week. Many then want to go further still and tackle a ten-day fast.

Fasting helps to put the body in its place—as the soul's servant not its master. The apostle Paul could probably have claimed not only to 'speak with tongues more than all' (1 Cor 14:18) but also to 'fast more than all' because he could write that throughout his apostleship he had been 'in fastings often' (2 Cor 11:27). It is noteworthy that he also puts 'fastings' (in the plural), high up his list of things which helped to mark him out as a true minister of Christ (2 Cor 6:4–5). How many ministers can put that on their CV?

We know from the many references in his letters that Paul was familiar with the Olympic Games and drew many illustrations from them. The way he refers to them in 1 Corinthians 9:24 'Know ye not that they which run in a race run all, but one receiveth the prize?' seems to sound in that opening phrase a definite note of

mutual reminiscence. Most probably Paul and the Cor-
inthian Christians witnessed among the spectators and
the athletes of the biennial Isthmian Games in AD 51.
(Shades of Seoul 1988 and the teams of Christians from
the Korean capital and from many parts of the world
whose only objective at the Olympics was to win souls.)
It is clear from the terms which he uses that Paul was *au
fait* with the boxing and wrestling as well as the field
and track events. When he says: 'I keep under my body,
and bring it into subjection: lest that by any means,
when I have preached to others, I myself should be a
castaway' (1 Cor 9:27) he is actually using a technical
boxing term (*hypopiazo*) which was literally 'I hit under
the eye with the fist'. That was the 'knock-out' punch
and in this case Paul said he used it on his own body to
beat it and defeat it and make it his slave. Paul did not
believe in beating about the bush or in beating the air
(v 26) or, as we would say today, in 'shadow boxing'.
Fasting was undoubtedly an exercise which Paul used
to help discipline his body and keep himself physically
fit as well as spiritually fit. I have a feeling that Paul
would have been very much at home at International
Prayer Mountain.

Paul Kauffman, the highly-respected missionary
leader of Asian Outreach, says: 'Korean Christians are
undoubtedly the prayer leaders of the Christian world.
Both the amount of time spent in prayer and the fervency and power of their praying sets an example for all
of us.' Paul Kauffman spent his high school years in
Korea and so he knows the land well. It is interesting,
therefore, that he suggests 'the famous Korean prayer
mountains may have their roots in the national culture'.
He thinks that

the prayer mountains are culturally derived from an attraction to the mountains which is a part of the Koreans' nature. Korea is one of the world's most mountainous regions. Mountain retreats for prayer were common in Korea long before the coming of Christianity. Both Korean Confucianism and indigenous Shamanism incorporated prayer and meditation in the mountains as an integral part of their practice.[2]

Whether that be so or not there is no doubt that the Christians have totally 'converted' those mountains and they are absolutely Christian prayer mountains. Their great virtue is that they are centres of concentrated prayer. It is their main business, their sole reason for being. They concentrate wholly on prayer and the thousands who flock to them do so to give themselves entirely to intercession. In such an atmosphere of concentrated prayer, by thousands of committed believers, every day of the year, it is not surprising that miracles of healing and deliverance are a regular occurrence.

The great virtue of fasting is that it concentrates our praying most wonderfully. Fasting enables prayer to focus more sharply on its objective. Fasting seems to be especially relevant when it comes to the realm of deliverance from demons in certain chronic cases, as evidenced by the words of the Lord Jesus himself in the incident of the deaf and dumb boy. Nine of his disciples had tried in vain to deliver the boy and it is clear from the narratives that they were acutely embarrassed by their unaccustomed failure. After all, they were not novices in this ministry of healing and deliverance. They had enjoyed great success in this area of the supernatural ever since Christ had first commissioned them as his twelve apostles and given them 'power against unclean spirits, to cast them out, and to heal all manner of sickness and all manner of disease' (Mt 10:1).

Hence their troubled question: 'Why could not we cast him out?' (Mt 17:19).

The timing of the incident is as illuminating as the answer—for Jesus had just been away for a few days at a 'prayer mountain'—subsequently famous as the Mount of Transfiguration. We are indebted to Luke, as we are so frequently when it comes to extra insights into the praying of Jesus and his teaching on prayer. The beloved physician mentions that the specific purpose of the trip was that '[Jesus] took Peter and John and James, and went up into a mountain to pray' (Lk 9:28). Furthermore, Luke reveals that it was 'as [Jesus] prayed, the fashion of his countenance was altered, and his raiment was white and glistering' (v 29). Jesus descended from that prayer mountain, having heard afresh the all-powerful voice of his Father in heaven. Peter's eye-witness (and ear-witness) account is particularly gripping:

[We] were eye-witnesses of his majesty. For he received from God the Father honour and glory, when there came such a voice to him from the excellent glory. This is my beloved Son, in whom I am well pleased. And this voice which came from heaven we heard, when we were with him in the holy mount (2 Pet 1:17–18).

Fresh from that glorious encounter with heaven in the mount, he was invincible. Jesus

rebuked the foul spirit, saying unto him, Thou dumb and deaf spirit, I charge thee, come out of him, and enter no more into him. And the spirit cried, and rent him sore, and came out of him: and he was as one dead; insomuch that many said, He is dead (Mk 9:25–26).

The answer of Jesus to his disciples' question is vital for it reveals that in certain cases faith needs the back-up of fasting and prayer:

> Jesus said unto them, Because of your unbelief: for verily I say unto you, If ye have faith as a grain of mustard seed, ye shall say unto this mountain, Remove hence to yonder place; and it shall remove; and nothing shall be impossible unto you. Howbeit this kind goeth not out but by prayer and fasting (Mt 17:20–21).

In spiritual warfare, when engaged in close combat with the powers of darkness, Scripture and the experience of countless mighty men and women of God who have been used in this ministry of deliverance down through the centuries, combine to emphasise the necessity of fasting.

Scripture makes it clear that there are degrees of authority in Satan's kingdom. 'We wrestle not against flesh and blood, but against principalities, against powers, against the rulers of the darkness of this world, against spiritual wickedness in high places [or against wicked spirits in heavenly places]' (Eph 6:12). Daniel is the classic example of this. After a life-time of experience in praying and in dealing with 'life at the very top' as prime minister under successive governments and rulers, as an old man he still gave himself to fasting and praying (Dan 10:2–3). For three full weeks he fasted and when at last a mighty angel visited him, this great heavenly being revealed that the reason for the delay in answering his prayer was opposition in the heavenlies. He said:

> Fear not, Daniel: for from the first day that thou didst set thine heart to understand, and to chasten thyself before thy God, thy words were heard, and I am come for thy

words. But the prince of the kingdom of Persia withstood me one and twenty days: but, lo, Michael, one of the chief princes, came to help me; and...now I am come (10:12–14).

In the last decade the Holy Spirit has been raising up a great army of intercessors all around the world to recover the ground lost by prayerless, lukewarm churches. The tide is already turning but at the fore-front of the battle are those who fast as well as pray. Yonggi Cho will tell you that he regards International Prayer Mountain as the front line of their attack on the Devil's forces on this earth. Probably nowhere else in the world can one find such a concentration of people praying and fasting—and, remember, there are also many other prayer mountains in Korea, all run on similar lines, though not as large.

The Hanul Mountain Prayer Retreat Centre has been the scene of some great gatherings for prayer and fasting. In 1980 Korean Christian leaders of several denominations called the millions of believers to join in a chain of prayer and fasting for forty days due to the critical political situation across the country. The emphasis was upon personal repentance and commit-ment and the need to lay hold on God for a nationwide moral and spiritual awakening. The climax was a three-day prayer and fasting rally at the Hanul Prayer Moun-tain from 28th February to 1st March, when more than 30,000 people gathered.

The Korean Christians are great lovers of the word of God and take this as their guide on all matters of faith and conduct. Dr Jashil Choi bases her teaching on fasting on the Bible and says: 'The basic element of this experience is faith in the unchanging word of God. The Bible, written under the inspiration of the Holy Spirit, is our only rule of life and faith.' (See 2 Timothy 3:16.)

Fasting is a positive way of expressing our belief that man is not just a physical being. Fasting is a faith acceptance of the truth that 'man doth not live by bread only, but by every word that proceedeth out of the mouth of the LORD doth man live' (Deut 8:3)—the very words with which Christ defeated the Devil at the end of his forty-day fast (Mt 4:4).

Fasting is putting food in its correct place. It is saying we eat to live—we do not live to eat. It is a balanced acceptance of the fact that we need food but there is something else even more important. Job put it succinctly when he said, 'I have esteemed the words of his mouth more than my necessary food' (Job 23:12). It is not going to unscriptural extremes of asceticism and punishing the body as though it were evil. The very opposite: correct fasting shows we appreciate that our bodies are wonderfully made and we seek to keep them healthy so that every faculty will be at its best for God's service. Dr Jashil Choi is very much a specialist on health foods which helps to put into perspective her balanced teaching on fasting. Balance is very important here. It is not the cure-all and end-all of everything. Korean Christians can feast for the glory of God as well as fast. Like the early church, they know how to 'eat their meat with gladness and singleness of heart' (Acts 2:46) as well as minister to the Lord and fast (Acts 13:2).

5

Fasting and Intercession

In 1984 when the Christians in Korea learned that the Olympic Games were to be held in Seoul in 1988 they immediately started praying. That special prayer meeting continued daily for four years. The target was not that Korea would win a lot of gold medals (although they did win a surprising number and passed many other nations including the United Kingdom in the medals table). Rather the aim was to win as many souls as possible for Christ. They saw the tremendous soul-winning potential of competitors and spectators from 163 nations gathering in their capital. The faith of the Korean church is that God will use them in world evangelism in a miraculous way. They saw the Olympics as God bringing the world to them and they seized the opportunity with both knees as well as both hands. They prayed and prayed, and fasted and fasted. But they did more: they prepared. They believe that you cannot do any more than pray until you have prayed, but after you have prayed then you can and must do more.

They prepared beautifully designed gospel leaflets in full colour in all the various languages of the competing nations. They not only gave them to all the competitors and spectators but in numerous cases they supplied key people with ample spare copies to take back with them to their own country. What a vision. What a task. What an accomplishment. Only eternity will reveal the full impact of Seoul '88. Those Korean intercessors will continue to pray for those who came to Christ and for their testimonies and literature as they penetrate deep into Russia, into the Arab strongholds of Islam in the Middle East, into Africa, South America, yes, and into darkest Europe! Korea's praying church is having an increasing impact on a needy world. Prayer mountains and fasting and united, targeted intercession are the spiritual weaponry responsible.

United fasting and intercession gets results—yes, even in backslidden Britain. A fortnight before Reinhard Bonnke's great Eurofire Conference in the massive Birmingham National Exhibition Centre (July 1988), my wife Hazel and I were privileged to attend a week of prayer and fasting (Monday to Friday) at a retreat in Staffordshire under the anointed leadership of Suzette Hattingh. The venue was the Elim Bible College at Nantwich. Although the invitation was strictly limited, the response was such that a second centre had to be booked for accommodation, and even then many had to be disappointed as both centres were filled to capacity. For the 240 of us fortunate enough to be involved it was an unforgettable experience.

In over forty years of fasting experience I found this by far the easiest. No doubt this was because it was group fasting and everyone was of one heart and one mind, and also, because during the daytime at least, we were all in one place! I am sure that this is also one of the secrets of Prayer Mountain. People who have previously found fasting difficult or well-nigh impossible when trying to do it alone at home, find that they can do it when part of a large group involved in real prayer.

Another great secret of the week at Nantwich was having the benefit of the inspiring leadership and teaching of a person such as Suzette Hattingh. This again must apply in the case of Prayer Mountain; it is the dynamic and committed leadership of Dr Jashil Choi which has brought it to the place it occupies today. I have had the privilege of interviewing them both, and I sense so much that is similar in these two wonderful women of God, even though they are separated by more than a generation and they are almost a whole world apart so far as upbringing and religious background are concerned. Suzette Hattingh was born in the Transvaal in South Africa in 1956; Jashil Choi was born in Korea in 1915. Suzette grew up on a large farm, the baby of a big family of nine. A real South African of many generations, her family stock was originally German and Dutch. She was brought up in an extreme section of the Dutch Reformed Church. Jashil was brought up a Buddhist without any knowledge of Christ until her remarkable conversion as a young teenager. Suzette's father was very religious and very strict but without any experience of personal salvation through faith in Christ. Suzette naturally grew up the same: religious but unconverted, although she did somehow feel the hand of God was on her life even as a child. Her mother told her she was different from her other children. For example, she would sit for hours with a children's Bible, but with any other book or magazine she was bored in a matter of minutes. At boarding school in the prayer meetings she was conscious of a great Presence and she would burst into tears though she did not know why and her schoolmates teased and mocked her.

Like Jashil, Suzette left home to train as a nurse and qualified in both general nursing and midwifery. Still in the Transvaal, she attended church on Sundays when not on duty. In accordance with the doctrine of the Dutch Reformed Church she believed strongly in pre-destination, but her hopes of salvation lay entirely in good works. In the last year of her general training she met a man and they were going to get married but at the last minute they broke up and this brought a lot of pressure into her life.

It was at this time that God began to speak very definitely into her life. As senior nurse she had to take care of the dying. In several instances the dying spoke of what they were seeing and two cases in particular made a great impact on her life. One godless man spoke of the pit into which he was slipping. This perplexed her and made her fearful. She began to question, 'Am I a Christian?'

She was nursing a lady suffering from terminal cancer. For a time this lady proved to be an extremely difficult patient. Then she had to go away for some special treatment and when she returned she was a totally different person. She told them the reason—she had met with the Lord Jesus Christ and had yielded her life to him. As she was dying she described what she was seeing and hearing. She told them of beautiful music and as she was describing heaven there came such a holy Presence into the room that Suzette was frightened. Then the woman turned her head and said, 'They are coming to fetch me,' and in a moment she was gone. All of this forced Suzette to ask many questions about what happens after death. Where do people go? Was she herself ready? But she dismissed it by trying to convince herself that as a member of the Dutch Reformed Church she must be a Christian.

Soon after this Suzette saw a poster which said, 'Five minutes after the Rapture where will you be?' The poster was in connection with special meetings to be held in a Pentecostal Church. In Suzette's home 'Pentecostal' was like a dirty word. Dutch Reformed Church members (especially of their extreme persuasion) would never dream of entering such a place. Nevertheless, Suzette decided that she must go to this meeting whatever the consequences. The preacher said his piece and made an appeal for people to accept Christ. Suzette responded and went forward, but it was just emotion. There was no life-changing experience and nothing happened as a result of it. She was not born again.

A few months later, however, she had an amazing dream. She was on night duty at the time and sleeping in the daytime. Suzette likes to make it very clear that growing up on a farm with five brothers, they made sure that she was not superstitious or easily frightened. The dream was a very vivid one about the Second Coming of Christ and the Rapture. She saw Christ appear in the clouds and he seemed to fill the very heavens. Suddenly there was a great sound like a trumpet and thousands of people were caught up into the clouds to meet Christ. Suzette also found herself rising into the air but she got stuck at the roof and she began to cry out: 'Help me, please help me,' but in the dream Christ slowly turned his back on her. As he did so, the clouds out of which he had appeared became a thunderstorm and there was lightning and thunder. She knew nothing about the thunder and lightning and the scenes described in Revelation. When she woke up she thought she had just had a nightmare and she got into her uniform and went on duty.

It was a busy and tiring night duty and she was exhausted when she returned to her room in the morning. She went to sleep and experienced the very same dream again. She woke up too frightened to go back to sleep. She decided to get up, dress and go out into the town. That happened for four days in a row until she was too frightened to go to sleep. Every time she closed her eyes the same dream recurred. In the end she was so desperate for sleep, so exhausted, that although she never took drugs of any kind, she took some very strong medicine to induce sleep, but still she found herself having the same dream. The next night she was off duty but she was too frightened to go to bed and she fell on her face and prayed, 'If there is a God and this is true, then please do something in my life.' Right there in her own bedroom Jesus saved her soul; she was born again. She was twenty-two years of age when that happened.

Immediately her life changed drastically. The joy of the Lord came into her life and with it such a peace that the fear of death was gone. There was no one around to tell her what to do next, no one to tell her which church to go to. But the one thing which had happened was that God had given her a great hunger for his word. As soon as she came off duty she would run to her bedroom and read her Bible. She had such a desire that she could not stop, so that she read it many times over.

After about two months, as she was praying that God would speak to her through his word, she found that every time she opened her Bible it was about baptism. She could not understand it at first—after all she had been baptised as a baby. She experienced a real battle over baptism. In the end she prayed and said, 'Lord, whatever you speak to me about I will do.' Again and again she found her Bible opening to Acts 2.

By now some three months had passed by and she became quite desperate and prayed, 'O Lord, please help me and show me what to do.' Almost immediately the phone rang. It was a nurse who had had to leave the hospital some months before because of bad behaviour. In the interim period she too had become a Christian and had also been filled with the Holy Spirit. The night before she had had a dream about Suzette Hattingh in which she also saw three numbers. They were both thrilled as they shared their experiences about how they had become Christians. As they were talking, Suzette said to her friend, 'I have one problem, and I wonder if you can help me. It is about baptism.' Although her friend lived some fifty kilometres away, she said, 'If you like, my father and I will come over immediately and talk with you about water baptism.' They came and talked and the outcome was that Suzette wanted to be baptised.

Throughout her whole life, Suzette had never hidden anything from her parents and she knew that she had to tell them first what she was going to do. When she told her father, in her own words, 'he hit the roof'. He was very angry and upset but nevertheless, she made up her mind that she must obey the Lord no matter what the price. Eventually she was baptised in a charismatic Baptist Church and the date of the service turned out to be the very one that had figured in her friend's dream about Suzette.

That church was quite a distance away and so she was only able to attend on rare occasions. On her days off she did not know where to have fellowship and so she just went to her room, locked the door, got on her knees and prayed and read her Bible. She learned directly from the word of God. Before her conversion no one was concerned about her spiritual well-being but now that she was born again, everyone was afraid that she was becoming fanatical and her friends and family began to phone her up and warn her about 'over doing it'. As she prayerfully studied the Bible she found that God was giving her an understanding. She developed a great love for the word of God and the Holy Spirit taught her the great truths of salvation and prayer. She read very few books other than the Bible (and that still applies). Such was her appetite for the things of God that she made very rapid spiritual progress. Though no one told her to fast she did so almost from the beginning. Prayer and fasting and a voracious appetite for the truth of God's word became the road to spiritual power in her life. It was soon apparent that she was a 'chosen vessel', and in common with others of that calibre, she often found God waking her in the middle of the night to communicate his secrets to her heart.

Within three months of her salvation experience, the Lord made it clear to her that she would soon be working full time in his service. A year later she left her nursing career and went out into the South African bush country to join other Christians engaged in a tract ministry. She idolised nursing, so it was not an easy decision and she took it only after much prayer. This was just as well because she received tremendous opposition and persecution from her family and from the hospital.

Her faith and consecration came under further testing because she found that all she was doing was sitting in a very tiny office for eight hours a day writing out addresses. Suzette is extremely tall and largely proportioned for a woman. Very robust, strong and energetic, she is an impressive person in every way. She proved her dedication by sticking this out for five months. After much prayer and fasting she felt that she should go and see an old man of God at a mission station in the area. He ran a Christian Correspondence School and it was agreed that she should join the work. Again it was not an easy passage. She found herself doing all the menial tasks on the station, even down to cleaning the toilets. When not engaged in this way she was out for nine or ten hours every day at people's doors, giving out tracts and witnessing. She did this for almost two years and God blessed her labours. She had the joy of winning some souls for Christ, and she especially found God giving her a deep love for the women in the area. God used her to start women's prayer groups all over the city and in addition God blessed and used her in the schools linked with the mines in the area. Above all, however, her burden for the women increased and she felt that this had to be her main area of work.

It was during this time that she first heard Reinhard Bonnke preach. She had no idea who he was and she just forgot about him until some two months later when she had reason to visit the office of internal affairs to get some things sorted out. She was with some friends and it so happened that Reinhard Bonnke was in the building at the same time. Her friends knew him and as they met in one of the corridors they introduced Suzette to him. As he shook her hand Suzette felt the power of God come upon her and the Holy Spirit whispered into her heart, 'I want you to pray for this man.' She went home and did just that, even though she could not actually remember his name. Faithfully she remembered him in her intercessions for over a year until she met him again.

She was invited to a crusade as an observer, because the old man on the mission station was helping part time with the follow-up at that stage. It was only when she walked into the tent that she discovered that the evangelist was Reinhard Bonnke. She did not say anything to him or to anyone else, but at the end of the crusade one of the black pastors came to he and said, 'Don't you want to speak to the women?' Suzette was taken aback because she then spoke little English—her native language was Afrikaans. However, he persuaded her to 'give just a little word'. That was her first sermon and there were just eighteen women present, but God healed a blind child in the meeting and the next day there were forty-five women present and some responded to the invitation for salvation.

When the next crusade was organised they asked her to help on a part-time basis and to speak to the women again. She had had no experience of preaching up to this time and so she simply sought God in prayer and gave the women what God gave to her. In effect, that remains her basic method to this day: she can only impart to others what God has made real to her.

By the time of the third crusade, Christ for All Nations asked her to join them full time. She felt reluctant as she was very happy where she was, but after seeking God in prayer she felt very clearly that this was God's will for her life and so she responded. At first she did the women's work. She preached to them in the morning and Reinhard Bonnke preached in the great crusade meetings in the evening. She joined them in 1980 and that was very much the routine until 1983, when she intended to resign because she wanted to do Bible smuggling. However, as she prayed about it God gave her 'an open vision' in which she saw herself kneeling at a chair, praying, and when the people walked into the meeting she walked out of the hall. (Suzette says she has had only a very few 'open visions' but she can remember every one of them vividly.) She knew immediately that this was God speaking and that she must not go. God confirmed it to her in remarkable ways. He even sent a man to Botswana from Harare to give her a confirming message that 'this is what God wants'.

Up to this time, Suzette did not realise that this kind of prayer to which God was calling her was really intercession. She shared her vision with her leaders and told them that in future her ministry had to be moved from the end of the crusade to the front. Their reaction was far from encouraging. 'Totally impossible!' they told her. The leaders could not see what she was sharing with them. However, Suzette believes in total submission to God's leadership and she did not rebel. She was already speaking to as many as 10,000 women in one meeting. God began to move in a miraculous way on her behalf as she began to seek God in various periods of fasting. She fasted for fifteen days, then twenty days, and even forty days, examining her heart to see if it was right and her motives pure.

When the time was right, God spoke to Reinhard Bonnke. It was the right time and the right setting. Suzette had just come out of a twenty-one day fast in which she knew that she had prayed the matter through. When she appeared, everyone was saying, 'Pastor Bonnke is looking for you...where have you been?' Her one desire was to go before the crusade commenced, find a room and pray alone. She never dreamed of teaching intercession to others. However, Reinard Bonnke told her that he wanted her to pray for the sick and this was to be before the opening of his new 34,000-seater tent. Suzette was overwhelmed and frightened at such a prospect. Nevertheless, she accepted the challenge and got a group of intercessors together and mobilised a chain of prayer to prepare the way for the crusade. That was all she anticipated at first. Then she felt that as soon as Reinhard Bonnke started to preach she should leave the meeting and go into her caravan and pray while he preached. He could not see this at first and so in the true spirit of submission she remained on the platform but prayed where she was sitting.

After the crusade he called her into his office and told her he wanted her to do this full time. God had spoken to him about it and now he could see the wisdom of it. It was Suzette's turn to be unsure and she shut herself away in a small room in her caravan with just a bed, a cupboard and a little table. She came out only every second day for an hour for a bath. She fasted for forty days and it was one of the most difficult fasts she had undertaken, but during it God gave her the full strategy for this wider ministry of intercession.

The usual procedure in Reinhard Bonnke's major crusade is that after the organisers have gathered the churches in a city together, they then divide the city into regions and Suzette then moves in with two of her co-workers into each region in turn to teach intercession. This takes place a month or more before the actual crusade.

A whole series of prayer meetings then take place from early morning onwards for two weeks as they seek to prepare a highway for God in the locality. When the crusade starts, then each region has a 'duty night' for which it is responsible for prayer which begins one hour before the crusade meeting and continues right through until the altar-call is finished. It is a flow of worship, prayer, short teaching and intense spiritual warfare,

sometimes alone and at other times together. She constantly supervises all that is happening, moving con-
tinuously among the various groups of intercessors and
sensing what is happening in the spirit world.

Since this kind of intercession was introduced into
the Bonnke crusades they have noticed a remarkable
difference in the level of the anointing of God's Spirit
upon the preachers. There has also been a marked
increase in the miraculous, as well as deeper conviction
upon those responding to the appeal.

As well as the week of prayer and fasting before the
Birmingham Eurofire meetings in July 1988, Suzette
organised a group of some 3,000 intercessors each evening in another hall during the Eurofire week. In the
daytime she conducted special seminars on intercession. All of these were packed to capacity, and in the
second repeat seminars people were almost fighting to
get in and were most reluctant to leave when told by the
stewards that no way could they be admitted as the hall
was full. Suzette's example and teaching on intercession
has revolutionised the praying of thousands of believers
in Britain already.

Her present vision and burden is that she believes
God has called her to raise an army of intercessors. On
one rare occasion, as she was fasting, God spoke to her
in an audible voice telling her that he had called her to
raise an army of intercessors from the body of Christ.
This was to be done some six to eight weeks before each
crusade. It is a ministry which is proving very satisfying
as well as very successful. Her burden is to motivate
Christians to pray. She believes the day is coming when
she will go to a place to minister to the body. All will be
devoted to the spirit of prayer and the Spirit of God
moving on a city. People will respond as the spirit of
prayer comes upon them and there will be a prayer

revival. They will see the need to travail to bring souls
to new birth. As they prevail in prayer they will go out
onto the streets in the power of the Spirit of God. There
will be the mass crusade and then revival.

Suzette Hattingh has not established a prayer mountain but the procedure and the principles behind her
strategy are very similar to those of Dr Jashil Choi.
Physically they are very different, Suzette is a giant of a
woman, Jashil quite small. But spiritually they are both
giants for God and demonstrating the power of God
through prayer and fasting in the Western world, Africa
and the Far East.

6

Prayer in the 'Fast' Lane

There are two open secrets behind the successful
praying of Dr Jashil Choi and Suzette Hattingh. One is
fasting, the other is the fullness of the Spirit.

It is Jude who gives us a marvellous phrase which
unwraps one of the great secrets of intercession. He
urges his readers to pray 'in the Holy Ghost' (v 20) and
he obviously expected them to understand what he
meant. It is also suggested that when Paul says that the
Spirit 'maketh intercession for the saints according to
the will of God' (Rom 8:27) the word used, *huperen-
tugchano* (to intercede for one) is a picturesque word of
rescue by one who 'happens on' (*entugchano*) one who is
in trouble, and 'in his behalf' (*huper*) pleads with
'groaning which cannot be uttered' or with 'sighs that
baffle words' (Denney). Alford says, 'The Holy Spirit of
God dwelling in us, himself pleads in our prayers, raising us to higher and holier desires than we can express
in words.' This kind of praying in the Spirit has been
aptly described as super-charged intercession.

During the week of prayer at Nantwich in July 1988
with Suzette Hattingh and the company of 240 prayer

warriors, there were times when we experienced the
reality of such Spirit-boosted intercession. Faith soared
to heavenly heights where anything seemed possible.
We felt a marvellous assurance that Satan and his
principalities and spirit-forces of darkness had to yield
as the Holy Spirit made the victory of the cross so real
and glorious to us. We knew that we were not fighting
for victory, but *from* victory. The Holy Spirit led us into
travail for the precious souls bound by demonic forces,
and for the helpless victims of drugs and drink, and for
the multitudes of 'lost and lonely people in our inner
cities. It is a tremendous and heart-warming occurrence when fasting, Spirit-filled believers experience
'praying in the fast lane'. Only eternity will reveal just
what was accomplished by the praying at Nantwich,
but those involved at the heart of Eurofire felt sure that
the tremendous response of souls coming to Christ and
the many miracles of healing and deliverance were
definitely linked. It was a vital factor, but obviously not
the only one because throughout the week at Eurofire,
Suzette Hattingh led thousands in concentrated intercession in another hall as Reinhard Bonnke and his
team conducted the great rallies in the main
auditorium.

To those who find fasting difficult it will be an
encouragement to learn that Suzette Hattingh did not
find fasting easy to begin with. When she first started to
fast it was solely because she felt that God was speaking
to her about it. She cannot recall reading anything
about fasting or anyone speaking to her about it. It was
as she was giving herself to prayer that the burden came
to fast. At her first attempt she only managed to do so
for two meals then she had to finish. This was in the
early days of her Christian life when she was still nursing. At her next attempt she struggled to go without

even one meal. Try as she might she found she could not fast for twenty-four hours. Then one day, when she was in a car with a Christian friend, she shared with him the difficulties she was experiencing in trying to fast and asked him if he would kindly pray for her. He prayed for her right there and then in the car. At first Suzette found no difference. Some two or three months later, however, she really felt the Holy Spirit speaking to her very definitely about fasting. Suddenly every scripture she read seemed to be about the subject. Then a book about it came into her hands and this proved to be of further help to her. She immediately launched into and accomplished a seven-day fast. (This was some time before she joined Christ for All Nations.) Over the next two years she went from fasts of seven days to forty days at various times as God led her. Since then, like Jashil Choi, she has taught many people the secrets of successful fasting.

Both of these godly women are only too well aware of the dangerous diversions that may distract the immature when starting a ministry of fasting. One of the first things the Devil will seek to foster is the temptation to feel proud that we have fasted for a week, or two weeks, or more. Dr Jashil Choi wisely says: 'We must realise that God will not forgive our sins because of our fasting. All are sinners and by our own efforts we cannot receive pardon even though we fast for many days. We can receive forgiveness of sin only by the power of the shed blood of his only begotten Son.'

We must never fast for show. That was the mistake of the Pharisees when they fasted, and Jesus exposed this in his balanced teaching on fasting and prayer in the Sermon on the Mount: 'When ye fast, be not, as the hypocrites, of a sad countenance: for they disfigure their faces, that they may appear unto men to fast' (Mt 6:16).

Fasting is a godward exercise of the soul, and when this is the case, Jesus promised: 'Fast...unto thy Father which is in secret: and thy Father, which seeth in secret, shall reward thee openly' (v 18).

Dr Jashil Choi, from her vast experience, has some more very wise words on the subject. Although I have read many books on fasting, I think these are unique. They show a real insight into the workings of the human heart (even of Christians), and reveal the depths of her own Christian maturity. She says:

> It is very easy for some to slip into fleshly manifestations during a time of fasting and prayer. The Holy Spirit always works decently and in order. Therefore, it is necessary to restrain the fleshly manifestations that might occur. As we truly seek the Holy Spirit, He will show us the difference between spiritual and fleshly manifestations. It is impossible for us to differentiate without the help of the Holy Spirit. When we fast and pray we must not only restrain our food and drink, but also fleshly manifestations.[3]

On the practical side of fasting, Suzette Hattingh finds it helpful to drink warm water rather than cold water during a fast. After a total fast of a week or more it is necessary to take care in breaking the fast. Happily there are now several good balanced books on the Christian market which set out very clearly the procedures to be adopted to avoid harm. Before embarking on a fast of any length it is important to study these techniques carefully. Suffice here simply to stress that breaking such a fast must be done gradually with diluted fruit juices, and the intake must be increased gradually over a few days, until it is safe to move on to suitable solid foods. Most people find breaking the fast more difficult than the fast itself and this applies in the spiritual realm just as much as in the physical one. Concerning this period, Jashil Choi says,

> Even after we have finished fasting, God has met our needs, and we are motivated by the Holy Spirit, we are not perfect. We will not be holy or perfect persons until we receive our new bodies in heaven. It must be remembered that we are still at war with Satan and must battle courageously as we did during the time of fasting. Anyone who becomes proud because of his fasting will easily fall prey to the temptations of Satan. We can keep humble before God only as we continue to pray daily and study the Word of God.[4]

Fasting is the normal thing at Prayer Mountain and notice that, significantly, it always seems to come back on to the Christian scene in every time of Revival. It certainly played a significant part in the first wave of the Spirit of God in the period after the end of World War Two. The decade between 1945 and 1955 saw the rise of a whole new generation of men and women exercising a definite ministry of signs and wonders. Many of them fasted and prayed for weeks at a time, including people such as T L Osborn and Kathryn Kuhlman. Fasting and the supernatural seem to be inseparable.

John Wesley was a strong advocate of fasting. He declared that 'the person who never fasts is no more on the way to heaven than a person who never prays'. As always, Wesley was very balanced on the subject. He taught:

> There is scarce any of the means of grace which men have run into great extremes than religious fasting. How have some exalted this beyond all Scripture and reason—and others utterly disregarded it; as it were, revenging themselves by undervaluing as much as the former had over-

valued it! Those have spoken of it as if it were all in all; if
not the end itself, yet infallibly connected with it: these, as
if it were just nothing; as if it were a fruitless labour, which
had no relation at all thereto. Whereas it is certain the
truth lies between them both. It is not all, nor yet is it
nothing. It is not the end, but it is a precious means
thereto; a means which God himself has ordained, and in
which therefore, when it is duly used, he will surely give us
his blessing.[5]

John Wesley regularly practised fasting, mostly of
the short variety. His custom was to fast twice a week,
on Wednesdays and Fridays, until three o'clock in the
afternoon. A whole host of names of some of the godliest
people in every era of the church readily come to mind
as those who exercised this discipline continually
throughout their Christian lives. The great Jonathan
Edwards wrote of David Brainerd:

The reader of that life will see how much Brainerd rec-
ommends the duty of secret fasting, and how frequently he
exercised himself in it; nor can it well escape observation
how much he was owned and blessed in it, and of what
benefit it evidently was to his soul. Among the many days
he spent in secret prayer and fasting there is scarcely an
instance of one which was not either attended or followed
soon with apparent success and a remarkable blessing in
special influences and consolations of God's Spirit, and
very often before the day was ended.[6]

The saintly Open Brethren leader, Robert Chap-
man, made it his custom to spend every Saturday fasting. He shut himself away from people in his workshop.
It was not all prayer and fasting, but a mixed time of
recreative activity with his lathe, as well as communion
with his Lord. A person who made an emergency call to

the workshop one Saturday reported that 'his face shone as the face of an angel'.

Pastor Hsi is rated by many as one of the greatest men of God that China has ever produced. He exercised an amazing ministry of deliverance among the opium addicts and demon possessed. It was the nineteenth-century equivalent of *The Cross and the Switchblade*. Fasting featured regularly in his ministry. One of the first severe tests he had to face was the deliverance of his own wife who had become demon possessed. The heathen watched to see what he would do. He called for a fast of three days and three nights, and gave himself to prayer. He laid hold on God and his promises and then went to minister to his distressed wife. He laid his hands upon her and in the name of the Lord Jesus he cast out the evil spirits. She was completely and permanently delivered. She became a Christian and a faithful partner to her husband in his mighty ministry. Whenever a crisis arose, or if he met with a difficult case which defied deliverance, his one remedy was to resort to praying and fasting.

Oswald Smith of Toronto was a great giant of God of this century, who died only a few years ago after a long life full of tremendous blessing and challenge. He proved the power of fasting in his own life. A typical extract from his spiritual journal reads:

> Spent the day in prayer and fasting. On Wednesday night at the prayer meeting I announced that we would set aside the holiday when most were in the parks and places of amusement, as a day of prayer and fasting unto God. So we met at nine this morning and prayed through until nine tonight. The time passed very quickly and was a great blessing to many. Our prayer was for an outpouring of God's Spirit. Oh, how the people prayed![7]

What more can I say? I could go on to write of Charles G Finney, George Whitefield, Jonathan Edwards, Dr John Lightfoot of Great Munden in Hertfordshire, Hudson Taylor, Madame Guyon, Rees Howells, William Bramwell, Smith Wigglesworth and a host of others, all of whom have left on record their witness to the effectiveness of fasting.

Fasting and healing are also closely linked at Prayer Mountain and every day they see people healed of serious diseases. It seems that fasting can often play a significant part in divine healing. There is a well-known incident in the early life of Smith Wigglesworth which illustrates the point perfectly. A man came to Wigglesworth's home in Bradford requesting prayer. He had a leg which was cancerous from top to bottom. When Wigglesworth touched it with his hand he found it felt more like a board than a leg. Wigglesworth left the man while he went into another room to pray and seek the face of God as to what he should do. As he waited before the Lord in prayer these words came to him, 'Go, tell that man to fast for seven days and seven nights and his flesh shall come again like a little child's.' He delivered this message to the man who accepted it as a word from the Lord for him and said that he would go home and do exactly what he had been told. Four days later, Wigglesworth looked out of the window and there was the same man, but instead of holding the railings and pulling himself painfully up the steps, he jumped up the steps and started running round the house like a little boy, shouting, 'I am perfectly healed!' He told Wigglesworth he was returning home to complete the seven-day fast but he wanted him to know what God had already done for him. Wigglesworth said that he used to pray much and fast, especially in the early days of his ministry.

It is very significant that one of the main reasons why people go to the International Prayer Mountain is to seek to be filled with the Holy Spirit. It is logical that there can be no 'prayer in the Spirit' until there has been successful prayer for the Spirit.

It is also very interesting that there are many similarities in the experience of Jashil Choi and Suzette Hattingh. Jashil Choi says:

> There is a need to concentrate our efforts on teaching pastors to fast and pray until they receive the power of the Holy Spirit in their ministry. Through the power of the Holy Spirit, the church of 150 will grow to 500; the church of 500 will grow to 1,000 or even 5,000 members.

She takes the classical Pentecostal stand on being filled with the Spirit, declaring:

> As we yield all to Christ, He will baptize us in the Holy Ghost and fire. We then receive power to live an overcoming life and have greater love for the Word of God, deeper love for others, and an intensified burden for the lost. The initial evidence of this filling is the fluent speaking in an unknown language that we have never studied. There must be a movement of the love of God and the working of His Holy Spirit. God wants us to fast and pray. Through yielded vessels flows the revival power of the Holy Spirit.[8]

Suzette Hattingh likewise lays great stress on the person and ministry of the Holy Spirit in successful intercession. She will tell you, 'Intercession is saying, "Lord, my spirit is here to receive a burden from you by the Holy Spirit." Then your spirit becomes the womb of God through which people are birthed into the kingdom. Love and compassion are other essential characteristics, and so is discernment. These gifts don't come naturally but emerge as you begin to seek God.'

Suzette's pathway to power in the Spirit was by no means straightforward and was not without its traumas. When she was a little girl on her father's farm she was involved in an accident with a combine harvester. Her arm got caught in the machinery and was permanently damaged, leaving it slightly out of proportion with the other one. Her friend and her friend's father who arranged for her to be baptised in water also talked to her about healing and miracles, dreams and visions, and the power of the Holy Spirit. Suzette says that was the first time she had really heard about the Holy Spirit. On the Saturday night before the Sunday on which she was baptised in water, they took her along to a Pentecostal meeting and she admits she was frightened. Nevertheless, she did not want to miss anything that God had for her and she prayed quietly in her heart, 'Lord if this is all true, then let a so-called message in tongues come.' A man then spoke in tongues and someone interpreted. This frightened her even more, but she prayed, 'Lord, if this is of you, let it happen again.' Immediately another man stood up and gave an utterance in tongues and another interpreted. The pastor then said, 'I think God is speaking to someone here.' Others around her also began to speak in tongues and some were weeping and Suzette began to feel she was in the wrong place. She did not know what to make of it all. The pastor then asked who wanted to receive the Holy Spirit, and Suzette, although still somewhat afraid, in her heart wanted all that God had for her and asked for prayer. The Pentecostal pastor was over-zealous and as he prayed loudly for her to be baptised with the Holy Spirit, he laid his hands upon her and shook her in his mistaken eagerness to get her to receive. All he succeeded in doing was frightening her completely.

On the Tuesday after being baptised in water, her friends took her to the little prayer meeting in the Baptist Church which was quite charismatic but not excessive. Suzette said she could take everything in these meetings except the raising of hands which she found totally unacceptable. However, in this prayer meeting the leaders knew that she had been frightened by what had happened in the Pentecostal meeting, and so they laid hands upon her very gently as they prayed for her to be baptised with the Holy Spirit. Almost immediately Suzette was 'slain in the Spirit' and found herself flat on her back. After that no one touched her but she felt as though someone took hold of her wrists and pulled her up onto her knees and raised her hands! She started speaking in tongues and remained in that position for a long time as she was filled with the Holy Spirit.

That night she had a double encounter. First she 'saw' God and then in what she describes as 'an open vision', that is with her eyes open, she saw Lucifer as vividly as if he stood in front of her. She started crying and calling upon God. It was the beginning of real spiritual warfare in her life of intercession. There is no doubt that the Holy Spirit's enduement of power brings us into immediate conflict with Satan and the powers of darkness. The difference is that, as people learn to intercede in the power of the Holy Spirit, they are taught how to bring them down and cast them out through the victory of the cross.

Prayer Mountain is a place of front-line warfare in the heavenlies against the denomic forces of evil and darkness. Suzette Hattingh drives this message home. These are the secrets of prevailing prayer in this realm which the Holy Spirit has taught her since she asked God to teach her how to pray. First, determination.

Half-hearted, double-minded, uncertain praying will achieve nothing. In spiritual warfare it is essential to pray with determination. Secondly, direction. Settle on your target and then pray with a clear focus in that direction. Thirdly, specifics. Suzette tells how the Holy Spirit taught her this lesson in the early stages of her walk with God. She prayed for a pair of shoes at a time when she had no money to buy any and the old pair had holes in the soles. How she prayed! A month later she was still praying and the holes in the old ones were getting bigger and bigger. Very discouraged she got down and prayed, 'Lord, have you seen what my shoes look like? I have asked you for so long for a new pair, and I really believe that you want to give them to me. Still I don't have them. Father, where is the problem?' She heard the voice of God very clearly, 'You never told me what kind of shoes you wanted.' Quickly she answered, 'Excuse me, Lord. I didn't know you wanted me to be so specific. I want a pair of black, patent leather shoes, please!' Within a week a lady came to her house and told Suzette that every time she closed her eyes to go to sleep, Suzette's face came before her and the Holy Spirit kept telling her that she must buy Suzette a pair of shoes. Suzette says it was her first lesson in being specific but it became a principle that she has since applied right through her Christian life. Many will recognise that this is very similar to the way the Holy Spirit taught Yonggi Cho in the early days of his prayer life the necessity of being specific. (In his case it was a bicycle and a desk and a chair.) Fourthly, faith. Believe and keep believing that it will come to pass. Expect and continue expecting that it will happen.

Spiritual principles along these lines are put into practice at International Prayer Mountain. People who go there are taught to be determined in their praying and that is one thing that immediately strikes you. They go determined to get their prayers answered. If they are praying for the Spirit's enduement of power, then they focus on that and lay hold on God, determined like Jacob of old not to let him go until he has blessed them. If they are praying for healing, then day after day they take hold in faith of God's promises for healing. They turn the promises into prayer and remind God of his own word. They pray unceasingly and it is claimed that some 70% receive the healing they came for. If they are praying for the salvation of their loved ones, then all their praying is directed to that end. They are very specific and will name the ones they are interceding for and will not leave until they have a definite assurance in their hearts that God has granted them their petition. If they are praying for revival then they will pray until faith rises in their hearts that they are going to see it in their church. They will then return confident enough to declare their faith that they are going to experience revival in their church and prepare for it accordingly.

One of the great advantages of prayer mountains is that because they are places where prayer is continually offered, there is an atmosphere of faith, hope and love. Because they are also places where prayer is constantly being answered, the testimonies inspire others to new heights of faith in their own praying. The result is that at prayer mountains it is not a question of a vicious circle of unanswered prayer but a victorious circle of constantly answered prayer that gets bigger and bigger all the time.

7

The Master's Mountains

In the Bible it is so easy to miss some tremendous truth
because of a chapter ending. This is especially the case
in the last verse of John chapter seven and the first verse
of chapter eight. When read together these two verses
give us an insight into the sacrificial and dedicated
prayer life of the Lord Jesus. 'And every man went unto
his own house. Jesus went unto the mount of Olives.' It
has been well said in commenting on these verses that
while most people in a strange town asked which was
the best hotel where they could obtain a bed for the
night, Jesus always asked where was the nearest mountain where he could get alone and pray. It would be
interesting to know just how many ordinary mountains
and hills in Israel Jesus turned into prayer mountains
during his life. Here are two which readily come to
mind: 'And it came to pass in those days, that he went
out into a mountain to pray, and continued all night in
prayer to God' (Lk 6:12). That was before he chose the
twelve apostles. 'And when he had sent the multitudes
away, he went up into a mountain apart to pray: and

when the evening was come, he was there alone' (Mt 14:23). That was after the feeding of the five thousand.

When it comes to prayer, Jesus is the supreme Teacher and Master of the subject. His praying was so attractive that, on one occasion when he came to the end of his prayer time, his disciples asked him to teach them to pray. Clearly, when Jesus interceded they felt the power of his prayer and they wanted to learn the secret of 'praying like that'. One secret was that he knew when to stop. We read on this occasion 'when he ceased [praying]' (Lk 11:1). Jesus warned against 'long prayers and vain repetitions'. The example he gave to his disciples—the Lord's Prayer—was also short. Even reciting it slowly takes less than forty-five seconds. George Whitefield remarked on one occasion when 'some good brother' was going on and on in his prayer: 'He prayed me into a good frame of mind—then he prayed me out of it!' While Charles Spurgeon, whose public praying was as notable as his preaching, said, 'There are those who pray for twenty minutes in the prayer meeting and then bemoan their "short comings"!'

We in the West are desperately in need of being taught again how to pray. The lessons are ready to hand, of course, and so is the Teacher—if we are willing to learn them and be taught by him. Consider, for example, that marvellous verse of Romans 8:26, 'The Spirit also helpeth our infirmities.' According to K S Wuest, the word 'helpeth' (*sunantilambano*) means 'to lend a hand together with and at the same time with one'. It depicts one person coming to another's aid by taking hold, with that person, of the load he is carrying. He is not taking the entire load but he is helping the other one carry it. This is exactly what Martha was asking for in the well-known incident with her sister

Mary when she asked Jesus, 'Bid her that she help me.' Martha may have been left in the kitchen alone (and with thirteen hungry men to feed, that was no small task) but we are never left in the prayer room alone. As soon as we begin to intercede and get under some God-given burden, the Holy Spirit comes to share the load with us.

A study of the teaching of Jesus on prayer in the parables in Luke's Gospel is extremely rewarding. In the story of the Prodigal Son we find an illustration of someone asking amiss for his own lusts or pleasures (15:12,13; cf Jas 4:3). In the same story we find a prayer that was composed by the prodigal but never uttered (ie 'make me as one of thy hired servants' v 19b). The case of the elder brother illustrates 'ye have not, because ye ask not' (Jas 4:2). His father never gave him a kid because he never asked for one. The inferrence of the father's reply is that his older son could have had a dozen fatted calves if he had wanted, all he had to do was ask, because all that the father had was his. What a lesson for us!

The parable of the Publican and the Pharisee in Luke 18 gives us a justifying prayer by the publican: 'God be merciful to me a sinner' (v 13). Did Jesus take this story from a real live incident? Is it possible that the publican who prayed like that was none other than Zaccheus, whose conversion story follows in the next chapter? Be that as it may, the publican in question gives us the only safe prayer for prodigals, 'God be merciful to me a sinner.' The Pharisee shows us a prayer that was no prayer. The elder brother and the Pharisee both got nothing because they asked for nothing. With the Pharisee it was all 'I ... I ... I'—five times he said 'I'. The elder brother is not far behind him with three 'I's' and a 'my'. The promise is, 'Ask and ye shall receive.'

The story is told of Johnny Oxtoby, or 'Praying Johnny' as he was called, of Primitive Methodist fame. He was in a prayer meeting when a man was praying at great length. The man adorned his prayer with flowery phrases and went all round the moon and all round the world without ever coming to the point. In the end Johnny could contain himself no longer and he interjected in his broad dialect. 'Ask for summat, man! Ask for summat!'

The twin parables of the man asking for bread at midnight in Luke 11 and the widow asking for justice from an unjust judge in Luke 18 were told to drive home the importance of persistence in prayer. Persisting in prayer until the answer comes is constantly demonstrated at Prayer Mountain. It shows how thoroughly they have mastered this basic essential and it is one of the great differences between their praying and ours. They pray persistently, positively, specifically and aggressively. We pray weakly, negatively, generally and passively.

These parables are twins but they are not identical. The first one emphasises the importance of importunate prayer for others; the second one emphasises the importance of importunate prayer for one's self.

The first one could well be called 'How barefaced cheek filled an empty larder', because 'importunity' (Lk 11:8) is literally 'shamelessness', 'barefacedness', or 'impudence'. If anyone less than Jesus had said this we would not have accepted it, but he is actually saying that what friendship failed to give, impudence won!

'A bare larder' is the first chapter heading of this bread-seeking saga. In the middle of the night a knock at the door of the first friend reveals a lost, lonely and hungry friend on the doorstep. (Lost because the marginal rendering of 'in his journey' is 'out of his way'. Weymouth translates it 'from a distance'. Was this some prodigal, starving with hunger, on his way home to his father's house?) It seems right to assume that he woke him up, but every knock of need must be answered. George Whitefield believed and practised that 'God never puts a need in our way but that he intends for us to meet that need'. Are we our brother's keeper? Yes, we are.

What should he do? Send him away? That is unthinkable. Or is it? The disciples did not think so when Jesus faced them with the task of feeding the five thousand. Their solution was, 'Send them away, that they may...buy themselves bread: for they have nothing to eat' (Mk 6:36). Jesus answered, 'They need not depart; give ye them to eat' (Mt 14:16).

The man doesn't want to send his friend away, but unless he can get help he will have to because he confesses, 'I have nothing to set before him' (Lk 11:6). His larder was as empty as Mother Hubbard's. Prayer springs from need. Need drives us to prayer. We are Mother Hubbards in a world of Oliver Twists— millions of them, always 'asking for more'. The truth of the matter is that we *have* nothing, we *are* nothing, we *can do* nothing of ourselves; but through prayer, we *can have everything*, we can be *something* and we can do *anything*. Prayer is for bankrupt nobodies.

The quest is for bread. Insensitive Marie Antoinettes are still glibly propounding, 'Let them eat cake,' but the need of the world, the need of hungry prodigals, is for the good, wholesome bread of the gospel.

The second chapter heading is 'the comfy bed'. The first friend fortunately knows of a third friend and even at midnight he sets off down the street to his house. He knocks and knocks until things begin to stir. Alexander Whyte, the great Scottish preacher, imagines the dogs beginning to bark, and lights going on and windows going up as neighbours want to find out who is daring to disturb the peace at this unearthly hour.

Nothing can deter this man, however, and he calls out 'Friend, lend me three loaves; for a friend of mine in his journey is come to me, and I have nothing to set before him' (Lk 11:5–6). The word 'lend' implies 'to give as a piece of business'. It has been well said that salvation is free but you have to pay for everything afterwards. Not with money, of course, but there is a price to pay. All who have mastered the art of successful prayer have paid a great price for it. Prayer is no game, nor is it a 'trivial pursuit' but rather it is the grand objective of a dedicated life. The apostles knew this and refused to be diverted, even to serve vital tables. Their grand pursuit was: 'We will give ourselves continually to prayer, and to the ministry of the word' (Acts 6:4). Prayer was their first priority, even before preaching. Prayer mountains are a sign that the church is rediscovering her priorities.

He calls him 'friend' but the initial response is anything but friendly. 'Trouble me not: the door is now shut, and my children are with me in bed; I cannot rise and give thee' (Lk 11:7). In other words, 'Don't bother me; I've locked up for the night and it is a lot of trouble to undo the door. I'm in bed and it's nice and warm, and the children are in bed and asleep. Woe betide you if you wake the baby. I can't be bothered to get up and go down to the larder.' But he never says that he has no bread and so he meets with an even more business-like refusal to go away or to be quiet.

Jesus does not say that God is like that, but he knows only too well that God seems so sometimes, especially when we are praying.

The man keeps on knocking and asking. He refuses to go away empty handed. He thinks of his hungry friend back at home and in spite of the barking dogs and the protesting neighbours and the crying baby, he brazens it out. He knows that at midnight the knocker usually wins.

The third chapter heading is 'a bare face'. Listen to Jesus, 'I say unto you, Though he will not rise and give him, because he is his friend, yet because of his importunity [his impudence, his barefaced cheek] he will rise and give him as many as he needeth' (v 8). At long last his asking is answered; his search ended; his knocking rewarded. The door opens and he steps from the darkness into the light; out of the cold into the warm; out of want into abundance. He asked for three loaves but I have a feeling that when his friend opened his larder and he saw its fullness he went away with more. God never gives us less than we ask for but he very often gives us more.

The three loaves may well represent the three basic requirements which most frequently occupy our praying. The salvation loaf, the bread of life, is the one needed by all prodigals as they return home to the Father's house. Never mind 'Mother's Pride', this—we may reverently say—is 'Father's Pride', produced at tremendous cost, but given freely to all who ask.

The healing loaf is the children's bread. In the story of the healing and deliverance of the Syrophenician woman's daughter we find Jesus very clearly saying that healing is the children's bread. It is their right, their inheritance. What nourishing bread it is too, for just a few crumbs which fell from the Master's table were sufficient to make this tortured girl perfectly well and whole (Mt 15:26–28). Everyone who engages in the ministry of divine healing soon finds that it is beset with problems and difficulties. It is a costly ministry and many abandon it. But at Prayer Mountain they have found that when people are as persistent and as determined as this Gentile mother, then God gives them not crumbs but full loaves, and large ones too. A visit to Prayer Mountain provides much food for thought on this thorny subject of healing. Their success rate makes me ponder whether the difficulty lies not so much in the doctrine of divine healing as in our lack of prayer commitment. It is surely significant that the context of prayer for the sick in James 5 is that of persistent and definite prayer and the illustration chosen by the Holy Spirit is that of Elijah's praying for rain, rather than his praying for the fire. Even Elijah had to pray seven times before the rain came after three and a half years of drought (v 17). James had a tremendous reputation in the early church as a mighty man of prayer. He is extremely forthright in declaring that whether we are asking God for wisdom or for healing, we must 'ask in faith, nothing wavering' because the ditherers and the double-minded will not receive anything of the Lord (Jas 1:5–8).

The fullness of the Holy Spirit is the third loaf, and a very satisfying one too. Listen again to Jesus' application of this parable.

And I say unto you, Ask, and it shall be given you; seek, and ye shall find; knock, and it shall be opened unto you. For every one that asketh receiveth; and he that seeketh findeth; and to him that knocketh it shall be opened. If a son shall ask bread of any of you that is a father, will he give him a stone? or if he ask a fish, will he for a fish give him a serpent? Or if he shall ask an egg, will he offer him a scorpion? If ye then, being evil, know how to give good gifts unto your children: how much more shall your heavenly Father give the Holy Spirit to them that ask him? (Lk 11:9–13).

If you have not yet experienced the ascended Saviour's throne gift of the 'mantling of power from on high' then ask. Put away all fear and frightening suggestions of well-meaning but mistaken people who will try to put you off by inferring that you might receive a demon. It is unthinkable, says Jesus in effect, that if you are a child of God and you ask for the 'bread' of the Holy Spirit's power, he would allow an alien spirit to invade your life. Multitudes of all denominations visit Prayer Mountain with this purpose of being filled with the Holy Spirit in mind, and very few, if any, return disappointed.

The twin parable of the widow and the unjust judge (Lk 18) again drives home the lesson of importunity in prayer, showing just how important Jesus regarded this factor in our prayers. At the same time this intriguing story takes us deeper still into the mysteries of prayer. The purpose of the parable is revealed in the introduction: 'And he spake a parable unto them to this end, that men ought always to pray, and not to faint' (v 1). The various modern renderings of this last phrase are helpful: 'Men ought always to pray and not to lose heart...never to give up...not to cave in.'

This lesson is absolutely vital when it comes to praying for the lost and especially for the unconverted members of our families. It is something they understand only too well at Prayer Mountain and it is thrilling to know that there are thousands of testimonies of those who have gone to pray for the salvation of their loved ones and God has answered.

I suspect that Johnny Oxtoby would have been very much at home at Prayer Mountain. On one occasion a devout Primitive Methodist lady of Driffield, called Mrs Petch, was having to endure great persecution from her unsaved husband. She prayed much for him without any encouragement and was tempted to give up, but Johnny was adamant, 'Thou must keep praying, my dear. The Lord will convert thine husband.' One night she returned home from the prayer meeting to find the door locked against her. But her husband could not sleep and at midnight he got out of bed and she had the reward of hearing him crying aloud for God to have mercy upon him and save him.

In this parable it is significant that it is a woman who is the principle character, and a widow at that. Chapter one could well be called 'An unpromising picture'. It is clear that Jesus deliberately set out to paint as dark a scene as possible. A widow in the East in those days was the most unlikely person to get any change out of a corrupt judge. The backcloth to the parable is also interesting in that it immediately follows a graphic description of the dark days which will immediately precede Jesus' Second Coming. He warns that it will be as bad then as it was in the days just before the flood, and in the days before God had to destroy Sodom. But we can pray during dark days and difficult times. The darkest hour is just before the dawn. There is much of the prophetic in this parable, both for Israel and for the church. The message of church history is that again and again revival has come in such times and just when it seemed that all was lost.

What a situation! An unjust judge who was unholy and unhelpful. As he described this man, 'There was in a city a judge, which feared not God, neither regarded man,' heads would have nodded in the crowd. They all knew of such a character. With their region under Herod's jurisdiction, injustice and corruption were the order of the day and inferior judges such as this one were everywhere. He was just about the last person on earth to help anyone—and a widow such as this was the least likely of all to get anything out of him.

Chapter two, however, is 'unwearying petition'. This was her only weapon. She had no husband to defend her. In the first parable, the man had nothing; in this parable, the woman had no one. She presented her petition to him saying, 'Avenge me of mine adversary,' but he paid no attention to her. When it says, 'She came unto him' (v 3) the Greek is in the imperfect tense which means she kept coming. As Weymouth puts it, 'She repeatedly came.'

Every day when this judge arrived at his office she was there waiting for him. Every night when he left the court she was still there, badgering, pestering, giving him no peace. In the end she really began to get to him, he said she was wearying him (v 5). Campbell Morgan suggests that taken quite literally the phrase implies 'lest she give me black eyes'. Black rings were beginning to appear under his eyes due to sleepless nights. I imagine his wife began to get worried for him; she had never seen her ruthless husband in such a state. Every night when he came home, she would put out his slippers and give him the equivalent of his Horlicks, but all to no avail.

What did the widow want him to do for her? Who was her adversary? The word 'adversary' means 'an opponent at law'. Someone had taken from her something which belonged to her. Peter leaves us in no doubt as to who is our adversary: 'Your adversary the devil, as a roaring lion, walketh about, seeking whom he may devour' (1 Pet 5:8). The Devil is a thief as well as a liar and he comes to steal and to destroy.

When this story is linked with the incident of the Shunammite woman in 2 Kings 8:1–6, it is extremely illuminating. This was the woman who had provided 'a prophet's chamber' for Elisha and his servant, in return for which Elisha had prayed for her, and God had blessed her with a son (2 Kings 4:8–17). Later, this was the boy Elisha raised from the dead (2 Kings 4:18–37). Some years later, Elisha had warned her that a famine was coming which would last for seven years and she should emigrate until it was over. When she returned she found that squatters had taken over her house and land, and she went to petition the king for their restoration to her. The king granted her request. He appointed an officer of the court to see to it that she got back everything she had lost. 'Restore all that was hers, and all the fruits of the field since the day that she left the land, even until now' (2 Kings 8:6).

When applied to Israel, many devout Bible students believe that Israel will one day have all the land that God promised then—from Egypt right to the Euphrates. Applied to the church, this is what is happening before our very eyes in the miracle of renewal. The church is recovering all that she lost through unbelief and apathy. The gifts of the Spirit are being restored. Miracles of healing and deliverance are being demonstrated by the church around the world. Through repentance and persistent prayer God is restoring the 'years the locust hath eaten'.

The final chapter in the parable is 'Unchanging provision'. The unjust judge was compelled to deal with the widow's case. She won because of her persistence, her refusal to give up. Jesus applies it by saying, 'Hear what the unjust judge saith. And shall not God avenge his own elect, which cry day and night unto him, though he bear long with them? I tell you that he will avenge them speedily. Nevertheless when the Son of man cometh, shall he find faith on the earth?' (Lk 18:6–8). If he came now, he would certainly find the kind of faith he is looking for at International Prayer Mountain, and also at the many other prayer mountains in Korea, Japan and Taiwan. And if he tarries, who knows that there may even be a prayer mountain in Britain.

8

Where Men and Mountains Meet

The nearest thing to a prayer mountain in Britain, according to my research, seems to have been Mow Cop of Primitive Methodism fame. Mow Cop is a 1,100-foot high peak on the Cheshire-Staffordshire border, on the northern edge of the towns and territory made famous in the novels of Arnold Bennett. The dramatic rock formation at the summit is called The Old Man of Mow, and is capped by a ruined tower known as Mow Cop Castle. This mini-monstrosity was built as a folly by Randle Wilbraham in 1760, and never served any purpose other than to feed the man's ego. However, there are those who say that the silhouette of the ruin now bears the resemblance of a man kneeling in prayer. For those with a vivid enough imagination to see it as such, it is a fitting memorial to the mass praying which took place there in 1807, which many claim 'birthed' the Primitive Methodist Revival.

The poet William Blake once said, 'Great things are done when men and mountains meet.' Such was certainly the case on Sunday, 31st May 1807 when thousands of zealous Methodists converged on Mow Cop

from the surrounding regions for 'a day's praying on the
Mow'.

The men chiefly responsible for this important happening were Hugh Bourne (1772–1852) and William
Clowes (1780–1851). These two men of God are now
accepted as the undisputed founders of Primitive
Methodism.

Hugh Bourne was converted in the spring of 1799
after a long search for the truth. He was an avid reader
and he read many books before the saintly John
Fletcher's *Letters on the Spiritual Manifestations of the Son of
God* were used of God to bring him to a saving knowledge of Christ. Almost immediately, as he saw the
spiritual darkness around him, there was born within
him a passion for souls which characterised him to the
end of his days. It was a conversion as real and dramatic as that of John Wesley himself. Bourne's own
account needs no embellishment:

> I believed in my heart, grace descended and Jesus Christ
> manifested himself to me. My sins were taken away in that
> instant and I was filled with all joy and peace in believing.
> I never knew or thought anyone could, in this world, have
> such a foretaste of Heaven. In an instant I felt I loved God
> with all my heart, mind, soul and strength, and I felt a
> love to all mankind, and a desire that all—whether friends
> or enemies—might be saved. I heard an inward voice
> saying, "Thy iniquity is forgiven and thy sin covered."
> Life, light, liberty flowed in upon my soul and such rap-
> turous joy that I could not tell whether in the body or not.[9]

Bourne started his ministry of personal soul-winning
among the rough and illiterate coal miners of Harriseahead, in the neighbourhood of Mow Cop, and he
quickly learned that the secret of successful evangelism

was prayer. Before this, the only Methodist in Harriseahead was a godly woman named Jane Hall. A weekly prayer meeting was established in her cottage and Bourne, who was painfully shy, found courage to pray for the first time in public. It was an important breakthrough.

Among his first converts was his cousin, Daniel Shubotham, a miner who had sunk down in life through drinking too much. His education should have ensured him a good position but influenced by the degraded community around him, he had indulged in a life of drunkenness, crime and violence. He was a boxer, a poacher and a gambler, especially at cards. An outgoing character, he was the very opposite of the shy, introverted Hugh Bourne. Daniel was not at all attracted to his cousin Hugh and described him as 'a timid bashful fellow and no company for anyone'. Nevertheless, many earnest conversations took place between them. After one such bout of witnessing, they parted and Hugh was very down-hearted, feeling that he had failed to make an impression upon Daniel. In fact, the very opposite was the case. Daniel afterwards said that 'every word went right through me' and it was on his way home that his conversion actually took place. He arrived home to find his card-playing friends waiting for a hand of cards with him. He boldly told them of his conversion, opened his Bible and started to read to them. That was too much for them and they departed very quickly, convinced that his religious cousin Hugh had disturbed Daniel's mental stability.

Daniel's life was transformed and being a natural extrovert he was quickly witnessing to all and sundry with dramatic results. In a very short time several of the most notorious characters in the district were also won to Christ and there was the beginning of a divine awakening. The new converts joined in the weekly prayer meeting at Jane's cottage. The meetings were limited to an hour and a half because, as miners, they had to be up very early in the morning for work. These new converts were on fire for God and found this all too short. One night as the leader ended the meeting, they protested in a good-natured way: 'We have not all had a chance to pray. Why couldn't we have gone on longer? Why did we have to break up so soon?' Daniel Shubotham, with a prophetic touch upon him, said, 'You shall have a meeting on Mow Cop some Sunday and have a whole day's praying, and then you will be satisfied.' That was in 1801. It was a great idea but its time had not yet come.

The subject came up several times over the ensuing six years, during which another key person was converted. William Clowes was eight years younger than Hugh Bourne. He was born in Burslem and his family was quite well connected. His mother's maiden name was Ann Wedgwood and she was related to the famous Josiah Wedgwood, the founder of Etruria, whose Wedgwood-ware had earned him the title of 'The Queen's Potter'. Her father, Aaron Wedgwood, was also famous in his own right as the manufacturer of the first chinaware at Longton, Stoke-on-Trent. Unfortunately, Ann's marriage was not a specially happy one, due mainly to the excessive drinking and other bad habits of her husband, Samuel Clowes. Their son, William, was apprenticed early to his famous uncle, Josiah, and proved to be an expert at his trade. Unfortunately, this was offset by his copying his father's bad habits, and he soon learned to 'gamble, drink, fight and swear with the worst of them'. He was also a brilliant dancer and won prizes for this.

At last, however, he too was wonderfully converted in an early morning Methodist prayer meeting, following a love-feast at Burslem Chapel on 20th January 1805. His conversion was dramatic and lasting. Describing his experience he said, 'Oh what a wonderful change! What words can express it? My dungeon flamed with light. I was like one let out of prison. My heavy burden was gone. My soul, before bound with strong chains of unbelief, was now completely free. Almost frantic with joy, I leaped and shouted aloud!' From the first he proved to be a man of profound faith, a gifted preacher and, above all, he was deep and passionate in prayer. The stage was now set, the principle characters were prepared, and two years later the idea of a day's praying on the Mow found its time had come at last.

The needed spark was supplied by the visit to Harriseahead in April 1807 of an independent Methodist evangelist called Lorenzo Dow. This man had just returned from a visit to America where he had witnessed the effectiveness of their camp meetings. He spoke so enthusiastically about them that Bourne decided to hold a camp meeting at Norton in August. He shared the idea with the group at Harriseahead and they were all in favour but they felt that it was too long to wait until August. 'Why not in the meantime have that day's praying on Mow, which has been our dream for these six years past?' they asked him. Shubotham immediately examined the preaching plan for the spring. Finding that 31st May was a possibility he immediately declared, 'That's the camp meeting day.' The response was unanimous. The group immediately gave themselves to prayer, faith rose in their hearts, and they departed confident that God was in both of these great ventures at Mow Cop in May and at Norton in August.

The news that the meeting on Mow Cop was definitely fixed spread so rapidly and received such warm support that even Bourne and his friends were staggered and he commented, 'The news flew through the country as if it had gone on the wings of angels.' The idea of a day's praying on the Mow captured people's imagination everywhere and the intervening weeks were filled with continuous prayer around the country for God's favour to rest upon this great prayer gathering. They especially prayed for favourable weather as it had been agreed that if the morning was rainy the meeting would not go ahead.

Clowes and other leaders were only too well aware that the Methodist authorities were not at all in favour of camp meetings. 'Such things may be all right in America but are out of order in Britain,' was the mounting sentiment of officialdom. Bourne and Clowes knew that they were in danger of bringing the wrath of Methodist leadership down upon their heads but they felt so sure that this was the right thing to do, and the right time to do it, that they proceeded.

Clowes was so anxious not to miss a minute of the great day that he arranged to spend the Saturday night at Daniel's house, as he lived close by the Mow. Although the Sunday morning of 31st May 1807 dawned rainy, cloudy and unpromising, Clowes set off in good time to be on the Mow for the agreed starting time of 6 am. Even so he found he was not the first. There were some people gathered behind the shelter of a wall and they were already singing. He immediately joined them and they prayed together.

Because of the uncertain weather at dawn, Bourne and others held back at first, wondering what to do. He

wrote subsequently, 'The morning proved unfavour-
able; but about six o'clock the Lord sent the clouds off
and gave us a pleasant day.' There was a fairly cold
wind but nothing could deter the faithful intercessors.
They came in droves, not only from the Potteries but
from Lancashire and Yorkshire and even from Ireland.
They knew there would be preaching but it was the
prospect of praying together in great numbers which
really drew them. These were stalwarts of intercession
who already knew the secrets of praying with that holy
violence which wrestles, as did Jacob, with the
Almighty and pulls lost souls from the Devil's grip.
They were princes indeed who through much praying
had power with God and with men.

These men and women of prayer wasted no time but
mustered quickly into disciplined and determined
groups like troops moving into battle array. Soon the
prayer leaders of the various groups were 'storming
heaven' and demanding an answer from the Almighty.
This was not a question of whispered prayers, presented decorously and daintily, but all-out spiritual
warfare. (These were the people who were soon to earn
themselves the nickname of 'The Ranters'.) Voices
were raised in prayer and fervent Amens and Hallelu-
jahs filled the morning air, driving home the earnest
petitions and drowning the songs of the birds. There
were no 'deathly silences' between the prayers, for no
sooner had one finished than another started. Indeed, if
one paused too long for breath, someone else would
start before the other had really finished. But there was
no disorder and the leaders handled the growing
crowds with a heaven-given expertise which ensured
that while the Spirit was not quenched, neither was
enthusiasm allowed to get out of hand.

When the moment was adjudged to be right a rough pulpit was built up from the rocks which littered the hillside and the preaching started. Not that the preaching signalled the end of the praying, indeed the very opposite! While the preacher was giving his message the 'prayer squads' gathered at a suitable distance away, to support him throughout with their burning intercession. These preachers were to gain themselves the description of 'the now preachers' a few years later when Primitive Methodism was forced into existence because of opposition. The preaching on this occasion had two main targets. To set on fire the hearts of all committed Christians who were there and to offer Christ to the unconverted and the curious who had come.

It was not long before the crowds were too big for one 'preaching stand', and so a second pulpit was quickly erected from the rocks and boulders on the site. There was no shortage of preachers who could preach with power and authority, but if a preacher seemed to be losing the anointing of the Spirit then the message was soon signalled from the pulpit area to the prayer squads for the need of more intense intercession.

Bourne moved around the area to superintend the proceedings. After visiting the second preaching stand he discovered a group of people some distance from the first stand who were praying with a man who had 'come under conviction'. By the time he got through the growing crowds and nearer to the first stand he found another group of intercessors praying with several potential converts who were showing real distress of soul as the Spirit of God convinced them of their need of Christ. After he had stopped with them a little while he could tell from the noise from the other group that the man they had been praying with had really entered into salvation and was praising God very loudly. Before very long, many in the second group were also converted and their mourning (over their sins) turned into rejoicing.

As soon as one preacher finished another was ready to take over in his place and so the preaching and the praying carried on without a break until noon. By this time the crowds had swollen to the point where a third preaching stand was called for. This was duly catered for at a good distance from the other two stands. The numbers were now up to many thousands and the atmosphere was tremendous. Bourne's account says,

> The preachers seemed to be fired with uncommon zeal, and an extraordinary unction attended their word, while tears were flowing and sinners trembling on every side. Numbers of them were convinced and saints were uncommonly quickened. The congregation increased so rapidly that a fourth preaching stand was called for. Thousands were listening with solemn attention; a company near the first stand were wrestling in prayer for mourners [ie sinners under deep conviction], and four preachers were preaching with all their might.[10]

The crowds began to disperse from four o'clock onwards but many stayed and prayed through until after eight o'clock in the evening.

Clowes said:

> The glory that filled my soul on that day far exceeds my powers of description. Much of the good wrought at this great meeting remains, but the full amount of that good, eternity alone will reveal; and myriads of saints and angels will everlastingly laud the Eternal Majesty on account of the day's praying on Mow Hill.[11]

The meeting on Mow Cop was so successful that during the afternoon the suggestion was taken up by Bourne that another such meeting should be organised in July, and this time it should be for several days. The dates finally agreed upon were 19th to 23rd July. Bourne issued a leaflet announcing the meeting in which he included an account of the wonderful results of the memorable gathering on the Mow on 31st May. The news was greeted with great rejoicing by the praying people whose hearts had been touched by the flame of revival, but by no means everyone was pleased at the prospects of another such gathering and opposition quickly increased.

A local magnate tried to get the second meeting stopped on legal grounds but he had not reckoned on the determination of Bourne, who immediately set off to walk over thirty miles to Lichfield to get the ground licensed under the Toleration Act. The registrar made things difficult by insisting that a building must be erected before he would grant the licence. Bourne returned and set about the daunting task of getting a wooden building of considerable proportions erected on the site. Very suitably he called it the Tabernacle. He also arranged for three tents to be put up similar to those used in the American camp meetings. The required licence was granted, much to the rejoicing of the growing army of intercessors, and to the dismay of the swelling ranks of their opponents.

Nothing, however, could now stop the onward march of these praying and committed people and the July meeting was another huge success. Vast numbers attended and the organisation was good. The Tabernacle and the tents were a safeguard against inclement weather, and fires and lanterns were arranged to warm and light the camp during the nights. It was virtually a prolonged repeat of that first gathering on Mow Cop. Once again there was much fervent praying and anointed preaching of the gospel. Clowes wrote of it: 'The influence that accompanied the Word was great and many souls were converted to God.'

Very sadly, within a matter of days, the Methodist Liverpool Conference of 1807 virtually outlawed all such gatherings when they delivered their verdict on camp meetings: 'It is our judgment that even supposing such meetings to be allowable in America they are highly improper in England and likely to be productive of considerable mischief and we disclaim all connexion with them.'

Within a year Bourne's name was removed from the Methodist membership roll. The history of the continuing camp meetings and the birth of Primitive Methodism is another story. We are concerned here only with Mow Cop as a prayer mountain. What is significant is that 100 years later, in May 1907, an estimated 100,000 Primitive Methodists gathered on Mow Cop to remember their roots—'a day's praying on the Mow'. They came not only from Arnold Bennett's territory of the five pottery towns, nor just from a little further afield from the 'Black Country', but they came from every part of the United Kingdom, and from as far afield as New Zealand and South Africa. Although denounced as zealots and ostracised from the classic Methodism of their day, history duly vindicated Hugh Bourne and William Clowes and their followers for their passionate praying and their passion for souls.

A national newspaper, the *Morning Leader*, reported on 27th May 1907:

Primitive Methodists, if they had sought all the kingdom for a meeting place that should symbolise their bluff and rugged faith, would have had to come to Mow Cop at last.

It is the very hill. But they had not to seek it. It came to them by inspiration. It is Rome, Canterbury, and Mecca to them, and more also.

The one sad note that I can find in all this is that in my reading once again of the fairly extensive reports of the Centenary Celebrations on the Mow in 1907, the three main pursuits and aims of the celebrations were listed officially as Evangelical, Educational and Financial—prayer was not mentioned in its own right. It is true that there was some praying on the Mow in 1907. H M Tomlinson in his *All Our Yesterdays* wrote of that May Sunday morning: 'The first arrivals were some Scotch adherents. They came at four o'clock to be in time for prayers at six.' In writing of prayers rather than praying, the writer betrays himself and reveals almost certainly how the mighty Primitive Methodists had already fallen. The accounts are full of great preaching and lively singing but little else is mentioned about praying. Yet in their own history the lesson was underlined by Bourne himself. In 1817 and 1818 he complained that the camp meetings were losing their power and that the converting work in them had almost ceased. This he attributed to the growing custom of holding the camp meetings 'almost altogether with preachings and cutting off the general praying services'. When prayer was once again restored to its rightful place at the centre of things, 'the Lord returned in mercy, restored the converting power to the camp meetings, and the circuit began to revive'.

On the occasion of the Triple Jubilee of Mow Cop in 1957, the saintly and universally respected Dr W E Sangster, then the General Secretary of the Methodist Home Mission Department, wrote more discerningly of that great day in 1807:

Like men moving into battle those devout men and women mustered for the fight. The praying squads formed. The prayer leaders opened the encounter. At the right moment the preacher mounted his cairn of stones and offered Christ to every unsaved soul. So the battle joined. The angels must have leaned out of heaven to watch the contest. When the Word seemed to flag the faithful signalled from the preaching stands to the beseeching prayer squads for a reinforcement of power and, ere the night fell on that never-to-be-forgotten hill, God had taken great glory to himself. Tired but happy those devout souls went home quite unaware that they had made history and that, in after years, one vital stream of Methodism would look back to that praying day as a time of spiritual rebirth and Mow Cop become a name of reverence all round the world.[12]

A quick scan of the past reveals a positive galaxy of historic occasions when individual men and mountains met. Space permits only the briefest mention but they are sufficient to establish that a multitude of mountains are silent witnesses to the power of prayer.

The godly and gifted Irish preacher, Revd Thomas E Hackett, in tracing the roots of Christianity in Ireland, wrote of their patron saint:

It was here in Ballymena almost 1,500 years ago, and on the adjoining slopes of Mount Slemish, a young captive, and slave boy of sixteen, later [to become] the great apostle of Ireland, Saint Patrick, poured out his heart night and day in prayer to God, seeking his converting grace for himself and the mighty power of the Holy Ghost for the conversion of Ireland, still almost entirely pagan, to the faith of Christ, to which even then during his six years of captivity he was led to dedicate himself.

How touching are his own words, as found in his confession, or autobiography, a little document in rude

Latin, but of surpassing interest, and regarded by the highest authorities as authentic, to be found in the Book of Armagh: 'Before daylight I used to rise to prayer in snow and frost and rain, and I felt no harm nor was there any sloth in me, because, as I now see, the Spirit was burning within me.'[13]

The famous and successful Welsh preacher, Christmas Evans, who was born on Christmas Day, 1766, reveals the secret of his power in the following incident.

I was weary of a cold heart towards Christ and His sacrifice, and the work of His Spirit—of a cold heart in the pulpit, in secret prayer, and in study. Fifteen years previously, I had felt my heart burning within, as if going to Emmaus with Jesus.

On a day ever to be remembered by me, as I was climbing up towards Cader Idris, I considered it to be incumbent upon me to pray, however hard I felt in my heart, and however worldly the frame of my spirit was. Having begun in the name of Jesus, I soon felt, as it were, the fetters loosening, and the old hardness of heart softening, and, as I thought, mountains of frost and snow dissolving and melting within me.

This engendered confidence in my soul and in the promise of the Holy Ghost. I felt my whole mind relieved from some great bondage; tears flowed copiously, and I was constrained to cry out for the gracious visits of God, by restoring to my soul the joys of His salvation; and that He would visit the churches of the saints, and nearly all the ministers in the principality by their names.

The struggle lasted for three hours; it rose again and again, like one wave after another, or a high flowing tide, driven by a strong wind, until my nature became faint by weeping and crying. Thus I resigned myself to Christ, body and soul, gifts and labours—all my life—every day, and every hour that remained for me; and all my cares I committed to Christ.

From this time I was made to expect the goodness of God to churches, and to myself. In the first religious meetings after this, I felt as if I had been removed from the cold and sterile regions of spiritual frost, into the verdant fields of Divine promises.

The result was, when I returned home, the first thing that arrested my attention was that the Spirit was working also in the brethren in Anglesea, inducing in them a spirit of prayer, especially in two of the deacons, who were particularly importunate that God would visit us in mercy, and render the Word of His grace effectual amongst us for the conversion of sinners.[14]

In two years, he doubled the number of congregations from ten to twenty, and six hundred new converts were added to his mother church.

Other Welshmen who wrestled and prevailed on other Welsh mountains were Daniel Rowlands and Rees Howells, to name but two. There are many others such as Saint Columba of Iona, the apostle to Scotland (who with his followers constantly retreated to lonely islands and mountains to pour out his heart to God), William Grimshaw, Thomas Walsh, Jonathan Goforth, and a host of others whose names are revered for many qualities but supremely for their praying. And fortunately for the church, there is a far greater company still of unknowns, who are known only to God. But their lonely wrestlings are recorded in heaven and will surely be revealed in that day, when the Father who saw them in secret will reward them openly before the angels and redeemed mankind.

9

God's Mountaineers

In the early 1980s Athur Wallis shared with me that he felt God had told him it was time to take the subject of revival off the 'back-burner'. Events have proved that it was a true word from the Lord. His great book *In the Day of Thy Power*, published way back in 1956, became a classic on revival. Now, after simmering quietly for some years, the revival pot is back where it belongs, on the main burner at the front of the stove, boiling and bubbling as never before in the post-war years. Arthur Wallis was suddenly called home to heaven in September 1988, in the midst of a prayer conference at Sheffield. He was one of God's spiritual mountaineers, ever seeking the higher heights of prayer and faith and always stirring others to join him. Now, on every hand, there is evidence of a thrilling increase in praying in the Western world. No longer are we talking about history but rather history in the making.

In several cities around Britain there have been growing prayer movements since 1986. As yet there is no prayer mountain in the UK but there is a mountain of prayer going up, creating an atmosphere in which anything and everything becomes possible.

In 1986 a group of leaders in Birmingham felt the burden to pray, and finding a ready response across the city they formed 'Pray for Birmingham'. For two years prayer rallies of a thousand strong were held, under the leadership of men like Rev Bob Dunnett, the Vice-Principal of the Birmingham Bible Institute, and Rev Nick Cuthbert (an Anglican, well known for his work in the Jesus Centre in that city and as an evangelist). These were implemented with prayer marches of several thousands in the city.

Bob Dunnett is a thoughtful academic and seemingly a most unlikely person to lead successfully a massive prayer movement. But God's ways are not ours and he makes no mistakes. As someone has pointed out, if Personnel Management Consultants had been called in to submit an analysis on the fitness of the twelve apostles for international leadership, they would almost certainly have rejected them all apart from Judas—'an exceptionally bright young man with a sharp financial brain, an opportunist, personable, politically smart and able to negotiate a good deal with any government. Should go far.... As for the other eleven we regret that we find ourselves unable to recommend them as suitable material for world leadership.'

God looks on the heart and Bob Dunnett has thought and prayed revival for over twenty years. God usually prepares his chosen vessels away from the public eye until the time comes when he is ready to reveal his handiwork. John the Baptist was a case in point, and of him we read, '[He] was in the deserts till the day of his shewing unto Israel' (Lk 1:80).

God also usually pairs people together, because 'two are better than one' (Eccles 4:9). The Lord Jesus sent

out his apostles in pairs. The same principle is underlined throughout the Acts where we find that although
Paul usually had a team around him, he always seems
to have had one special person as a partner. Hence we
read of Paul and Barnabas, then Paul and Silas. Frequently it seems that the pairing is as unusual as the
type of individuals chosen. I feel it would be pre-
sumptuous of me to make any personal comment about
the pairing of Bob Dunnett and Nick Cuthbert. However, a nationally known leader and a friend of both of
them, in the presence of some thirty leaders as we were
praying specifically for them in their leadership role
with 'Pray for Birmingham', declared openly: 'You are
the most unlikely pair for such a role but the Lord has
brought you together for this task.' That was only his
opening 'salvo' but, I can tell you, it caused a sharp
intake of breath around the prayer circle! He then went
on with a prayer, richly mingled with prophetic input,
which found a clear witness in our hearts. A few minutes later we emerged onto the platform at the Birmingham National Exhibition Area for an evening of
'Prayer and Praise Proclamation'. The great arena was
filled to capacity with over 11,500 people who had
accepted the invitation to 'come and pray for revival in
the heart of the nation'. It included the national pre-
mier of Graham Kendrick's *Make Way for Christmas* but
the whole evening was geared towards prayer for
revival, praise, worship, spiritual warfare and evangelism. That, in my humble opinion, is an excellent balance and seems to represent the coming together of the
various streams which the Holy Spirit has been empha-
sising in the last few years.

Graham Kendrick has been involved with Bob Dunnett and Nick Cuthbert from the beginning of 'Pray for
Birmingham'. Graham's leading of the worship was

superb, as usual. Bob and Nick shared the leadership of the extended prayer times for revival and did so with such a sure touch of God upon them that we were left in no doubt as to who had brought them together. That was on 16th November 1988. Note that date well, for I believe it will prove to be one of considerable significance in the coming revival.

The NEC Arena had been booked for the whole of that day. The morning and afternoon sessions were for Christian ministers and leaders to seek the face of God in earnest prayer for revival in the nation. It was a thrill to see the body of the arena filled and people spilling over onto both sides. There were over 5,500 Christian ministers and leaders present from all the major denominations and groupings. The programme was balanced and well planned. It included personal testimony on revival; teaching on revival; heart preparation for revival; supplication and praise proclamation. The bulk of the time, however, was rightly given to prayer and intercession.

The keynote statement of the object and intent of this great gathering could only have been written by people who mean business with God, and by people who have made it their business to seek God and to learn the secrets of revival from the word and from history. It stated:

> The intention is to make clear from the start the purpose of the meeting: it is not a general prayer meeting for various activities that are to take place in the country; it is not just an expression of unity in prayer. It is to be a clear and solemn invitation for God to move on the nation in extraordinary power and in a way transcending any efforts currently being organised—the object is to seek God for an extraordinary awakening and for an awakening that will be nothing less than national.

The invitation is made on the basis of

NEED	(we desperately need it)
DESIRE	(we really do want it)
FAITH	(we really believe God wants to refresh and save. We really believe God moves in extraordinary outpourings of the Spirit)
UNITY	(we have come together from all over)
HUMILITY	(we have nothing to offer but the mercy and grace of God).

One of the many highlights of this great day of praying came when all the leaders on the platform were asked to join hands and the whole gathering prayed for the unity of the body of Christ.

A moving moment followed this when a note was passed up to the platform. It said, 'We are charismatic Catholics and we are praying for revival and we are sad that there was no Catholic representation on the platform.' Bob Dunnett was able to inform them that there was a Catholic presence on the platform in the person of Charles Whitehead, a leader in the Roman Catholic renewal. (His testimony to his personal experience of the baptism in the Holy Spirit appeared in *Renewal* magazine in September 1988.) Charles Whitehead was baptised in the Spirit in 1976 and has maintained a fearless but loving witness in Catholic circles ever since. However strong the prejudices of Protestants are, only the most bigotted will refuse to acknowledge that the Holy Spirit is penetrating every section of Christendom. In a day of prayer such as this we soon become aware that we all have a great deal of repenting to do, whatever denominational label we may wear. No section of the church has a monopoly on God and God will not be constricted by any barriers men may raise. His all-seeing eyes are still constantly searching the earth and he will, as ever, show himself strong on behalf of any whose hearts are perfect towards him.

The very fact that such a meeting took place on 16th November 1988 at all was a witness to the over-ruling providence of God. On Saturday, 19th March 1988 the 'Pray for Birmingham' leaders had convened a long planned day of prayer in the arena. On that occasion they had booked the vast arena with not a little trepidation. Their funds were low and the whole idea of booking such a place for a prayer meeting seemed almost ridiculous. However, they felt so certain that they had the mind of God on the matter that they went ahead and booked it. Their vision had sharpened very definitely into prayer for revival and they issued a national call to prayer for revival. Graham Kendrick shared their burden to declare the lordship of Christ in Britain.

They felt that if 8,000 responded it would be really wonderful. They were absolutely staggered when so many responded that they not only filled the great arena but had to book an overflow hall as well. Finally, some 15,000 people came together on the memorable occasion. Bob Dunnett says of that day: 'The grip on the meeting was quite extraordinary and we knew undoubtedly that we had a mandate from God to continue. We felt a clear witness in our hearts that the next step we should take was to issue a call to ministers and leaders to gather together for a day of prayer for revival and spiritual awakening in the land.'

The meeting was only planned in April 1988 and the chances of being able to book the NEC Arena at such short notice were virtually zero. However, in a completely full NEC diary there was a cancellation, and so it was that Wednesday, 16th November 1988 was secured—and booked at a very reasonable rate. Even so, it was a major step of faith. To organise a national meeting on a Saturday is one thing; to do it mid-week is another. The vision was of gathering some 6,000 or more ministers and leaders from all sections, seeking God humbly and boldly for revival. It was felt that such a gathering would constitute a major spiritual breakthrough—and such it proved to be.

Another highly significant event also took place on Wednesday, 16th November 1988—the fourth Annual National Prayer Breakfast at Westminster. This was strictly by invitation only. The gathering of around 600 included not only ministers and leaders of all denominations, but committed Christians from the House of Lords and from Parliament, including the speaker of the House. It is gratifying to know that there is an increasing Christian commitment and penetration right at the political heart of Britain.

Future historians may well decide that these two great days, 19th March and 16th November 1988, should be ranked alongside those days of praying at Mow Cop on 31st May and 19th–23rd July 1807.

It has been heart-warming to witness a similar prayer movement developing in the city of Bristol where I wrote this book. This started at about the same time as the one in Birmingham, although until the spring of 1988 there was no contact between those involved in the two cities. An interdenominational 'core-group' of leaders in Bristol functioned for several years and organised some very successful city-wide Christian celebrations in the Colston Hall. In 1986 it was felt the time had come for a change of emphasis and the new burden was for prayer for revival. Invitations were sent out to ministers and leaders across the city and a whole series of very successful prayer breakfasts and prayer mornings was organised. An average of fifty ministers and leaders gathered in a variety of venues. One of the first was held in a city board-room on the top of a tall office block, which afforded us a panoramic view of the heart of this historic city. The key aspects of the life of the city became the focal-point and target for special prayer and spiritual warfare. Other prayer mornings were held on some of the sprawling estates in the city which have proved notoriously difficult for Christian work. Another memorable extended prayer gathering took place on the City Road in the St Paul's area—a district which gained adverse publicity world-wide when the race riots erupted there in the early 1980s.

One important climax was reached on Friday evening, 12th February 1988, when over a thousand gathered for an evening of intercession and spiritual warfare. Arthur Wallis was the invited speaker and he spoke on 'taking the city by spiritual warfare'. There was also plenty of victorious worship but the greater part of the evening was spent in prayer. As a result of this, several new interdenominational prayer groups were brought into being across the city, with the common purpose of praying for revival.

An extremely vital morning of praying took place on Monday, 12th September 1988, in the Bristol City Council Chambers. It required something of a miracle to get permission to hold a prayer meeting there, but praying in such places, with a local councillor and others involved in the life of the city present, ensures that a healthy note of realism pervades the praying. On this occasion it was an added blessing to have Rev Bob Dunnett there and his presence forged a new prayer link between Bristol and Birmingham, as well as a growing awareness of the increasing prayer power across the nation.

Dr Clifford Hill is another of God's spiritual mountaineers. Academically he is both a sociologist and a theologian. Spiritually, he is regarded by many as a modern-day prophet. The magazine *Prophecy Today*, which he launched in 1985 and of which he is the editor-in-chief, has now established itself as something of an élite publication in its particular field. A steadily growing circulation in a highly competitive market is testimony enough.

In 1986 he created quite a stir in Christian circles when 153 people, from forty different countries, gathered at Mount Carmel during Easter week to seek the face of God in response to his call 'to prophets from every land to come together and seek God's face in order to proclaim God's word to the nations'.

Elijah for ever established the reputation of Mount Carmel as one of the great prayer mountains of all time. With great courage, Clifford Hill had no set agenda, no timetable and no list of speakers for this unusual occasion. He left it as unstructured as possible 'in order to allow God to speak to them'. For one period of twenty-four hours they 'went into silence, observing a fast of words'. At another time they all went to the site where Elijah confronted the prophets of Baal in the great natural ampitheatre on Carmel. The whole international company then proclaimed in their own languages the lordship of Jesus. This was followed by prayers being said over the land in Hebrew and Arabic by local Christian leaders.

People of spiritual repute who were present at Carmel 1986, and with whom I have conversed, have all confirmed that it was an occasion they will never forget. It is one which has left an enduring impression on their lives and ministries. The impact of people and reports from the Third World countries which are experiencing revival was considerable. The Christian leaders from the West felt that God was saying very powerfully to the churches there: 'Take your hands off *my* church. Let *my* voice be heard. Let *my* face be seen and let *my* word be heard. "Not by might, nor by power, but by *my* spirit," says the Lord Almighty.'

Mount Carmel at Easter 1986 became a prayer mountain once again. Real spiritual warfare was waged against the forces of evil and darkness which are threatening to engulf the world. Those present report that there was deep searching of hearts and much repenting as the Spirit of God revealed how the divisions in the church grieved God. Tears flowed and hearts were melted.

Dr Clifford Hill's message has been constant over the last few years. His main emphasis is this: 'The key that releases the blessings of God into the world is repentance. It is repentance that breaks the power of the enemy and enables the power of God to flow through the nations.' He affirms that 'repentance must begin at the household of God for that is where judgment will begin'.

There was another prayer mountain in Elijah's life, after Carmel, and that was the Mount of God—Sinai, the place where God was revealed in his awesome holiness as a consuming fire. It was there, after fleeing from Jezebel, that a humbled and broken Elijah was recommissioned. One of the powerful messages preached at Carmel 1986 apparently centred on the theme that Elijah's main lesson was learned at Sinai not at Carmel. 'The lesson is that we are no earthly use if we cannot hear the voice of the Lord. Although earthquake, fire and storm came, God did not speak through them, but through the still small voice.' Unless and until that happens, a prayer mountain is just another mountain, a heap of rock. It is when we are in a place and condition to hear 'that still small voice—God's voice of gentle stillness', causing us to 'wrap our faces in our mantle' that an ordinary mountain is transformed into a prayer mountain and we are transfigured into a little more of his likeness.

10

Why Can't We Have a Prayer Mountain?

Many devout believers in the West are asking, 'Why can't we have a prayer mountain here?' Before we can answer that there are several other questions which should be answered.

'Are prayer mountains scriptural?' Is there really authority in the New Testament for a place to be specially set aside for prayer? Does not the very concept contradict the answer of Jesus to the Samaritan woman at Jacob's well? She asked: 'Our fathers worshipped in this mountain; but ye say that in Jerusalem is the place where men ought to worship.' He replied:

> Woman, believe me, the hour cometh, when ye shall neither in this mountain, nor yet at Jerusalem, worship the Father.... The hour cometh, and now is, when the true worshippers shall worship the Father in spirit and in truth: for the Father seeketh such to worship him. God is a Spirit: and they that worship him must worship him in spirit and in truth (Jn 4:21,23,24).

Can we not pray with equal effectiveness anywhere and everywhere? The answer to that must be 'yes'.

However, we find that even the Lord Jesus himself found some places especially conducive to prayer, such as Gethsemane, where he 'oft-times resorted' (Jn 18:2).

'Would a prayer mountain really work in our culture—are they essentially a part of Eastern tradition and basically a 'hang-over' from Buddhism?' Certainly the idea is less strange to the orientals and there can be no doubt that it is much easier to establish prayer mountains in the Far East than in the Western world. The fact that there are literally dozens of prayer mountains in Korea is proof of this.

'Would a prayer mountain ever be accepted in Britain with its still strong Protestant traditions? Are not prayer mountains just a half-way stage to Catholic monasteries?' There is no doubt an element of danger that within one or two generations a prayer mountain could degenerate into a place that savoured more of superstition than of the genuine supernatural where the power of God was manifested. I used to wonder how on earth the church could ever have moved from the Acts of the Apostles to the superstition of the Middle Ages with its veneration of relics and pilgrimages to shrines. It seemed totally incomprehensible to me. However, in my own lifetime I have witnessed the fall of a few Pentecostal evangelists. Happily they have been few and they have been the exception not the rule. I am persuaded that some of them were men of God, men of prayer, who started out with a tremendous anointing upon their lives. There is no doubt whatsoever in my mind that they experienced many genuine conversions and were used in the working of some outstanding and authentic miracles. But how are the mighty fallen when, for example, one such independent, American evangelist (long dead, let it be said), virtually 'sold' or put on 'offer' to those gullible enough to send him their money, 'little squares of canvas from his miracle tent', which was being replaced with a new one—with the 'promise' that they could expect a miracle of healing when they received it.

Dr Martyn Lloyd-Jones shrewdly observed that 'Christian people tend either to be guilty of great ostentation or else to become monks and hermits. As you look at the long story of the Christian Church throughout the centuries you will find this great conflict has been going on.' In the same message he also dropped another pearl of wisdom: 'Evangelicalism is not only something in and of itself; it is always, in addition, a reaction against Catholic teaching. The tendency of a reaction is always to go too far.'[15]

The fact is that all the successful prayer mountains in Korea belong to red-hot, deeply committed Protestants of the evangelical persuasion. The world-famous Young Nak Presbyterian Church in Seoul, the largest Presbyterian Church in the world, is very much in the Reformed Protestant tradition. It was founded in 1945 by the godly and prayerful Dr Han Kyung-Chik. Their present pastor, Dr Park Cho-Choon, says:

Many Korean churches have a prayer mountain or retreat centre where groups and individuals can go for prayer, Bible study and meditation. Our church also has a prayer centre on the northern side of Seoul which is used by many of our members. I truly believe that our church is growing because people are sincerely praying.[16]

The same applies to the Kwang-Lim Methodist Church in Seoul (the largest Methodist church in the world). The Senior Minister, Dr Kim Sun-Do, is a Methodist of the old evangelical tradition, and he has recently established a prayer mountain in connection with his church.

As yet a healthy balance has been kept in the running of these prayer mountains in Korea. Up to the present they have been preserved from becoming a snare to this praying people. Of course, as David du Plessis was fond of declaring, 'God has no grandchildren—only sons.' The snare will only come if another generation grows up and takes over, who are not 'born from above', and who are just Christians by tradition and not by regeneration.

The saving factors in the Korean prayer mountains are that they are all connected with churches which are not only evangelical but evangelistic. There is a difference: 'Evangelical is the truth on ice; evangelistic is the truth on fire.' They are essentially prayer retreats where committed Christians can go aside for a day, or a week, or even a month. Then they return to their normal work-a-day life. Only a small staff are long-term residents and they are not left to their own devices but are part of the mother church and its discipline and supervision.

Our spirituality in Western evangelicalism still tends to be measured in terms of ceaseless activity. The Protestant 'work-ethic' is deeply ingrained in our very culture; most of us feel guilty if we are not doing something and working hard. The idea of drawing aside and simply waiting on the Lord is still foreign to many Protestants.

I was brought up a Protestant in the old Methodist traditions and I can still remember the rift caused in the wider family circle when one of my cousins married a Catholic. Such a thing was unheard of in the Whittaker family. We could trace our Methodist pedigree back to the 1830s. None of our family attended the wedding. For years after that we hardly ever spoke to that branch of the family.

Even now it is not easy for me to acknowledge that there is a depth and quality of devotion in some charismatic Catholics which is all too rare in Protestant circles. Is God seeking to redress this imbalance? Have prayer mountains and prayer retreat centres a part to play in this? It is worth remembering that the noted Brethren leader, Sir Robert Anderson, almost a century ago dared to write:

> Surely we can afford to be sensible and fair in our denunciation of the Church of Rome. Who can fail to perceive the growth of an antichristian movement that may soon lead us to hail the devout Romanist as an ally? With such, the Bible, neglected though it be, is still held sacred as the inspired word of God; and our Divine Lord is reverenced and worshipped, albeit the truth of His Divinity is obscured by error and superstition.[17]

One of the most significant happenings in the last twenty years was surely the edict by Pope John which encouraged Catholics to read the Scriptures for themselves. It has resulted in a new interest in the Bible in Catholic circles and a new willingness on the part of Catholic theologians to study the Scriptures. Centuries of 'mind-set' is giving way to a new openness which is refreshing and hopeful. The danger is that in some Protestant circles the 'mind-set' not only remains but is hardening, refusing to accept or even examine anything which savours of renewal or restoration. As Dr Clifford Hill says, 'It is repentance that breaks the power of the enemy and enables the power of God to flow through the nations.' Will we Protestants, evangelicals, Pentecostals and Restorationists continue to nod approvingly at the repentance in Catholic circles, while feeling no need of repentance ourselves? Prayer mountains are excellent places for repentance. One of Yonggi Cho's simple remedies, if he finds one of his young pastors creating problems, is to send him up to Prayer Mountain for a week. Such people seldom return the same. Repentance after all is basically 'a change of mind leading to a change of heart and life'.

The number of prayer mountains outside of Korea is growing. There are several prayer mountains in Japan. Through the inspiration of Yonggi Cho one was set up in Taiwan just two or three years ago. As yet I have been able to trace only one in the West and that is in America in Louisville, Kentucky. It is connected with the Evangel Christian Life Centre and was established by the pastor, Wayne Rodgers.

There are, however, a growing number of churches with prayer towers, where prayer is virtually continuous. One very successful one is that which belongs to a church in fellowship with American Assemblies of God in Florida, called 'The Carpenter's Home Church', and located on Carpenter's Way, Lakeland. It is pastored by Karl D Strader who has exercised a very fruitful ministry there for several years. He has built the church up to the place where it now has a regular congregation of several thousand—and growing.

Karl Strader has kindly described the running of their prayer tower.

Our prayer tower is manned by prayer warriors around the clock. One of our men is responsible for gathering volunteers to take shifts and they are very faithful in this. If they are unable to keep their commitment, they call someone to take their place.

We have a picture file of the families of our church on this floor and they are prayed over by the prayer warriors. We have pictures of our staff and our missionaries so that these can be prayed over also. Lastly, we have prayer cards which come from our congregation, people who phone the church, people who phone our radio station, people who phone as a result of watching our television programme, and other sources. These are prayed over for a week and then rotated out.

This programme has been very effective in the promotion of prayer in our church and in providing opportunities of service for many people. We have approximately one hundred and seventy prayer warriors at the present time and many people have been helped through this ministry as their testimonies bear out.

In August 1988, the Colne Valley Community Church, along with other Christian groups in Colchester, made national headlines when they announced that they were 'relying on prayer in a property deal'. They said they believed that God was leading them to buy the disused Victorian Water Tower, the city's highest landmark, to convert it into a twenty-four-hour prayer tower. Working under The Network Trust, an umbrella group for several churches in the area, they needed to raise over £100,000 within a week to complete the deal.

The project started in 1986 when Pastor Peter Prothero of the Colne Valley Community Church and a handful of Christians in Colchester began to meet and pray together. Pastor Prothero says, 'During one of these meetings somebody got a picture in their mind of Colchester from the air. As we prayed we got the sense that God was drawing our attention to this tower, the highest point. When Jesus looked down on Jerusalem and wept it was from a high place, the Mount of Olives.'

Two months later the Anglian Water Authority announced that the water tower, built in 1882, was to be sold. It was a listed building but a property development company bought it hoping to obtain planning permission for a scheme they had to develop it into offices. When the necessary permission was not forth-coming they offered it to the Christians for £157,000. An initial deposit of 10% was required. They decided to pray, and if they could raise the deposit of £15,700 they would take it as a sign that God intended them to proceed with the purchase. The deposit was quickly raised. The test of faith came in raising the remaining £151,300. God met the need and the tower is now theirs. Raising the money, however, was probably the easy part, the real test of their faith and commitment will come in the task of establishing and maintaining it as a round-the-clock prayer tower.

The centre at Ashburnham Place, in Sussex, has also attempted to maintain a round-the-clock prayer com-mitment over the last ten years. Edmund Heddle was the instigator of this prayer project. He has been a Baptist minister for some thirty-seven years and served as the Chairman of the Ministry Main Committee of the Baptist Union of Great Britain and Ireland. Until the spring of 1988 he was the Warden of the Ash-burnham Stable Renewal Ministry. Christians of many denominations have regularly gathered at Ashburnham Place to pray for revival.

It was hoped that Dr Jashil Choi, the founder of the Yoido International Prayer Mountain in Korea, would be able to visit Britain in 1989 with a view to stirring up interest in the establishing of a prayer mountain. Due to unforseen circumstances this visit has now had to be postponed.

The great thing is that there is almost certainly more serious praying being done in Britain today than at any time since the end of World War Two. It would be 'interesting', to say the least, if a prayer mountain could be established in Britain. The vital thing is that God's people everywhere are responding to the call to prayer.

Thank God for the many women's groups around the nation who have been earnestly seeking God for the last twenty years. One of the best known of these is the Lydia Fellowship which was established some twenty years ago by Shelagh McAlpine, the wife of Campbell McAlpine. Chris Leage is now the national co-ordinator and Shelagh McAlpine is still involved. The Lydia Prayer Fellowship has spread around the world and there are approaching 4,000 involved in Britain. Their prayer emphasis is on intercession for the church and nation.

Shelagh McAlpine, looking back over the twenty years, says:

> We always proclaimed the Lordship of Jesus Christ in the meeting at the outset and much time was spent in worship, waiting on God with the Word, meditating on a passage, seeking God for insight in prayer and sharing and receiving from one another. God used our eyes to weep, our spirits to travail and our hearts and minds to persevere.

Bible meditation and fasting continue to be a central part of the Lydia programme. That, after all, is the heart of a prayer mountain.

Prayer mountains are not an end in themselves, but a means to an end—namely world evangelism, proclaiming the lordship of Christ to every living person. There is a growing commitment among Christians in many lands to make the 1990s a decade of world evangelism. At a recent meeting of Assemblies of God leaders from many nations, Yonggi Cho urged that Assemblies of God people should unite in a real commitment to pray together as a worldwide fellowship. My prayer is that the whole body of Christ will unite in prayer as never before for the evangelisation of the world.

Prayer is the key. Prayer, that is, in all of its many and varied aspects. As Paul puts it, 'Praying always with all prayer and supplication in the Spirit, and watching thereunto with all perseverance and supplication for all saints' (Eph 6:18). Goodspeed translates it: 'Use every kind of prayer and entreaty, and at every opportunity pray in the Spirit.' The harsh truth is that all of us have so much more to learn about praying.

'From the day of Pentecost, there has been not one great spiritual awakening in any land which has not begun in a union of prayer, though only among two or three; no such outward, upward movement has continued after such prayer meetings have declined' (A T Pierson).

In the concluding chapter of his classic on revival, *In the Day of Thy Power*, Arthur Wallis wrote:

> The appalling need of this hour is only matched by its unique opportunity to afford a display of the power and glory of God. Many a faithful intercessor of the past has desired to see the things which we are about to see, and has not seen them. In His matchless grace, God has brought us to the kingdom for such a time as this. The Saviour calls us to follow His steps in the pathway of intercession.

In the last year of his life, Arthur Wallis wrote:

> There is a bigger wave coming. God birthed us with the vision of it. Though it tarry, we wait for it—not just for the survival or enlargement of restoration, but for the blessing of the whole church and the bringing in of God's kingdom.[18]

There is a conviction among many praying people that we are on the verge of the greatest revival of all time. There have been many revivals. We speak of the

Welsh Revival and the Korean Revival and the Congo Revival, but we are waiting for the World Revival. This gigantic wave which is already beginning to roll in, is going to encompass the whole world and the whole church. God so loved the world that he gave his son—for every tribe and tongue and nation in it; and Christ so loves the church that he gives himself to ceaseless intercession for every truly born-again, blood-bought believer who is a part of it.

Mountains are rather thin on the ground in the British Isles. But when people really begin to commit themselves to praying and fasting, they can make mountains out of molehills! They are lifted to a higher place where 'all things are possible'—even worldwide revival and the quickening of the entire body of believers.